KEY GUIDE

Australian
Mammals

KEY GUIDE

Australian Mammals

Envirobook

Leonard Cronin

Illustrated by
Marion Westmacott

Leonard Cronin, is one of Australia's foremost natural history authors. Trained s a biologist, he is a prolific writer of books and articles on the Australian flora, fauna and the environment, bringing his own fascination with the natural world to the general reader. Among his other works are The Australian Flora, The Australian Animal Atlas, Ancient Kingdoms and Natural Wonders, Koala, Presenting Australia's National Parks and The Illustrated Encyclopaedia of the Human Body.

The illustrator of this volume, Marion Westmacott, is one of Australia's leading botanical illustrators. She works as a scientific illustrator at the Royal Botanic Gardens in Sydney.

First Published in Australia in 1991 by Reed Books
This edition first published in 2000 by Envirobook

Planned and produced by
Leonard Cronin Productions

Published in Australia by
Envirobook
38 Rose St, Annandale, NSW 2038

National Library of Australia Cataloguing-in-Publication Data:

Cronin, Leonard.
Key Guide to Australian Mammals

Bibliography
Includes index.

ISBN 0 85881 172 3

1. Mammals - Australia - Identification
1. Title

599.0994

Publisher: Leonard Cronin
Design: Robert Taylor
Additional research: Gertrud Latour
Printer: Kyodo Printing Co, Singapore

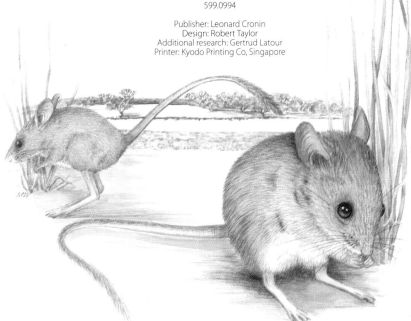

Contents

Preface
to the second edition

The first edition of *Key Guide to Australian Mammals* proved to be extremely popular and filled an important niche as both a field guide and reference book to our native mammals. The past few years have seen a resurgence in interest in the Australian fauna, and recent studies have revealed many new details about their lifestyles, habitats and distribution, and also clarified a number of anomalies in their taxonomy. This new edition incorporates scientific name changes and new facts that have come to light. Some new illustrations have been added by Marion Westmacott, and I have included information about animal traces—often the only signs of an animal's presence, and a valuable aid to identification.

Leonard Cronin, 2000.

Introduction

The Australian mammals continue to fascinate and surprise biologists as research gradually reveals more about their adaptations, lifestyles and behaviour. Isolated from the rest of the world for many thousands of years, they have penetrated even the most remote and inhospitable parts of the continent, surviving on the meagre food sources of the arid regions, developing strategies to deal with bush fires, droughts, high summer temperatures and freezing winters. In the past two centuries they have been faced with successive invasions of introduced species, destruction of their habitats and the encroachment of civilisation. Some, like the Grassland Melomys, thrive in association with mankind, reaching pest proportions in sugar cane plantations. Others, like Leadbeater's Possum, retreat to the few remaining patches of old, unlogged forest and watch helplessly as the bulldozers and chainsaws approach.

Over the millennia their strategies for survival have produced such unusual animals as the Platypus, equipped with a sixth sense to detect the minute electrical signals emitted by small aquatic invertebrates; the Marsupial Mole, which `swims' through the desert sands; and the magnificent Red Kangaroo, perfectly adapted to the arid interior with its fast, energy-efficient hopping gait and ability to survive for long periods without drinking.

Australia is the only country where the three types of mammal—marsupials, monotremes and placental mammals—exist side-by-side. While all suckle their young on milk produced in the female's mammary glands, they differ in the state of development of their newborn. Monotremes (the platypus and echidna) lay eggs with a leathery shell, while the placental mammals (rodents, bats and marine mammals) give birth to fully-formed young. Marsupials (kangaroos, possums, cuscuses, wombats, koala, bandicoots and the carnivorous marsupials) produce very small, incompletely-developed young. Some marsupials suckle their young in the security of a well-developed pouch, while others offer the newborn little protection, dragging them around while they cling helplessly to the mother's teats.

Most Australian mammals are active during the night and around dawn or dusk. Many live in trees, and some possums have a membrane between the forelimbs and hindlimbs enabling them to glide. Bats have modified limbs with large flight membranes giving them the freedom of the skies, while other mammals have adopted a fast hopping gait, or taken to the water where they use flippers instead of feet.

Australia's hot arid interior supports many mammalian species that hide from the sun by burrowing into the ground. They can survive without drinking by producing highly-concentrated urine and dry faecal pellets, obtaining sufficient free water from their diet or by the chemical breakdown of carbohydrates.

Despite this wonderful variety of form and function, no comprehensive field guide to the Australian mammals has previously been published. The many thousands of bushwalkers, students and naturalists are faced with the unenviable task of lugging around large heavy volumes and struggling with difficult key systems, or trying to identify a species from memory.

In producing this field guide it has been my aim to help the interested observer to both identify and understand something of the lifestyle of our wildlife. Unlike human beings most Australian animals are shy and cryptic in their habits and do little to modify their environment. Many make their homes in tree hollows, conduct their daily lives under cover of darkness and leave few tracks and traces of their existence. Yet they often have quite complex social systems and remarkable adaptations that allow them to survive in harsh and hostile conditions. Within the limitations of the space available in a field guide I have attempted to give the reader an up-to-date knowledge-base that will satisfy most field requirements and encourage further reading and research.

The information is presented under sub-headings for ease of access. A simple visual key refers the reader to specific pages in the book where positive identification can be made using the illustrations, distribution maps and descriptions. Measurements are intended to give a guide to the relative size of an adult animal, and where possible the animals on a page have been illustrated in proportion to each other. Habitat descriptions indicate the general areas in which the animal is known to live. Many other factors determine their ability to survive, such as appropriate food sources, access to suitable nesting holes in old trees, the type of soil, temperature fluctuations and the presence of other species. The shaded areas on the distribution maps only show where the animal is likely to occur, given an appropriate habitat. The Latin names used are those currently accepted by the scientific community. However, these may be subject to change as research reveals different affinities, or subspecies are determined to be separate species in their own right.

One of the greatest challenges

facing the people of Australia is to learn how to coexist with our native wildlife. In our struggle to achieve economic wealth we have failed to consider the requirements of the animals we share this continent with. We destroy their refuges by cutting down ancient forests, then create new habitats with introduced plants and animals. A few native species may proliferate and become pests, but the vast majority disappear altogether or flee to the few remaining natural habitats where they are forced to compete for space and food.

Part of the problem lies in a lack of basic knowledge. The study of our native fauna has never been well-funded, and consequently we know little about the biology and habitat requirements of some of our most common animals. It is interesting to note that this lack of knowledge has been used as a defence by governments, companies and individuals to excuse crimes committed against the environment. Some of these have been far more devastating in their consequences than many crimes committed against society; yet in our justice system the perpetrators of social crimes cannot use ignorance of the law of the land as an acceptable defence.

If we devoted a fraction of the amount of time and money spent on litigation to understanding and upholding the law of nature, we would be able to look forward to a world with a secure future for all our native fauna, rather than watching the list of extinct and endangered species grow longer and longer.

How to use this guide

The following keys have been designed to make the identification of an unknown animal as simple as possible. The reader is guided to specific pages in the book where animals fitting the categories described in the keys are grouped together.

The boxes in the keys show a single animal or group of animals with similar characteristics. The numbers in the boxes give the pages where these animals are to be found.

The first page of the key describes the monotremes and sea mammals which are quite distinctive and easily categorised.

The second and third pages describe the majority of other mammals grouped according to their size. The small mammals are divided into carnivorous marsupials, rodents, possums, potoroo and bettong, rat kangaroo, bandicoots and bilby, and the marsupial mole.

Carnivorous marsupials have a long jaw with a continuous row of teeth.

Rodents have a more bulbous jaw and a long gap between the single pair of large upper and lower incisor teeth and the grinding molars.

Possums are mostly arboreal marsupials with a long, flexible tail, a quadrupedal gait and usually one or more teeth between the incisors and grinding molar teeth of the lower jaw.

The **potoroo** and **bettongs** can be distinguished from the bandicoots and bilby by their fast bipedal hopping gait.

The **bandicoots** and **bilby** have a rather graceless, quadrupedal, galloping run, short tails, pointed faces and coarse, stiff hair.

The last page of the key describes the bats. Examine the head and tail area and compare it with the diagrams in the smaller boxes. If it does not correspond to any of these categories, then it will most likely be found under **Other Bats**.

Monotremes and Sea Mammals

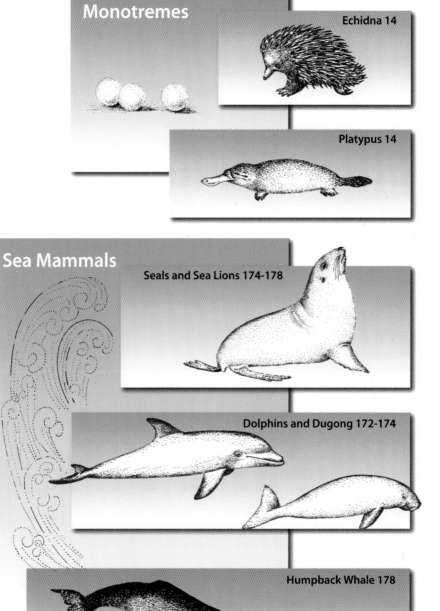

Monotremes

Echidna 14

Platypus 14

Sea Mammals

Seals and Sea Lions 174-178

Dolphins and Dugong 172-174

Humpback Whale 178

Small Mammals

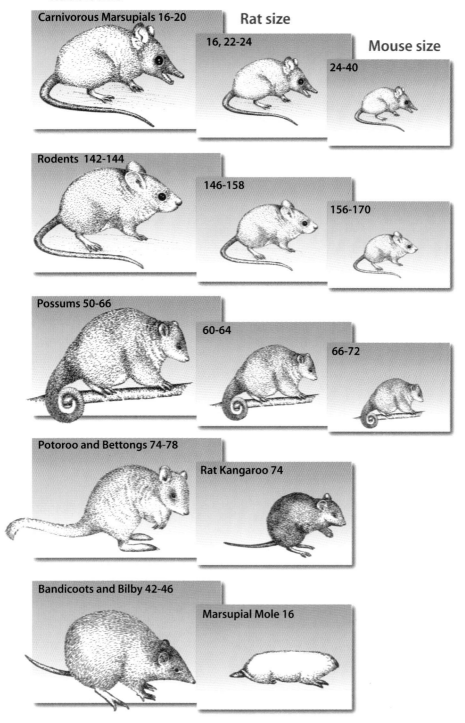

Rabbit size

Carnivorous Marsupials 16-20

Rat size

16, 22-24

Mouse size

24-40

Rodents 142-144

146-158

156-170

Possums 50-66

60-64

66-72

Potoroo and Bettongs 74-78

Rat Kangaroo 74

Bandicoots and Bilby 42-46

Marsupial Mole 16

Large Mammals

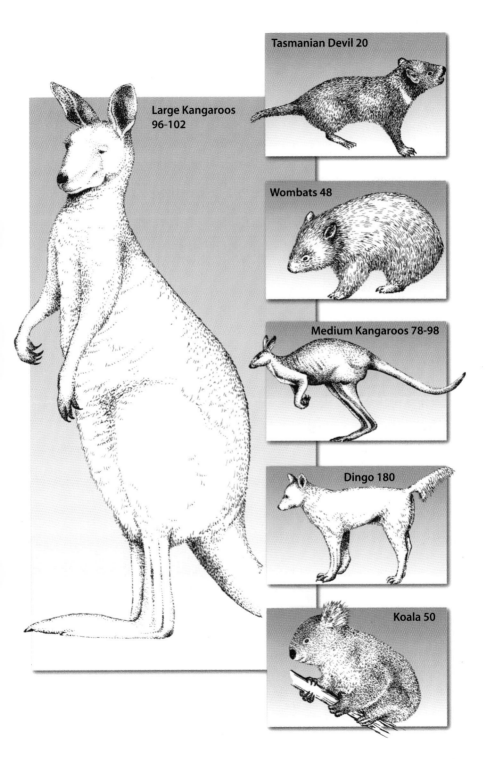

Large Kangaroos 96-102

Tasmanian Devil 20

Wombats 48

Medium Kangaroos 78-98

Dingo 180

Koala 50

Bats

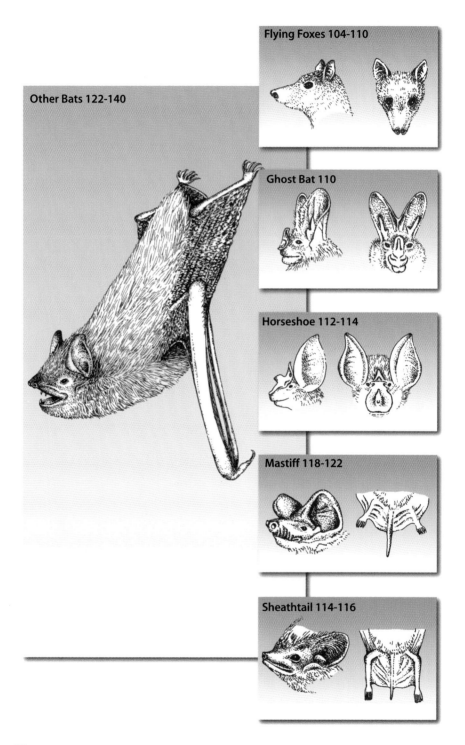

Flying Foxes 104-110

Other Bats 122-140

Ghost Bat 110

Horseshoe 112-114

Mastiff 118-122

Sheathtail 114-116

Illustrations and Descriptions

Short-beaked Echidna

Tachyglossus aculeatus

An egg-laying mammal with stout sharp spines on its back and sides, a tubular snout, a long, sticky tongue, small eyes and a rudimentary tail. Fur is dark-brown to sandy and often obscures the spines of Tasmanian animals. The spines moult annually and are creamy-coloured with dark tips. The short, powerful limbs have spade-like claws on the forefeet for digging and long claws on the hindfeet for grooming. Males have a small spur on the ankles of their hindlegs. **Behaviour** Usually active by day, they forage for up to 18 hours, probing with the snout, finding ants by smell and by their tiny electrical signals, detected by special receptors in the snout. They sleep under bushes, in hollow logs, rock crevices, Rabbit or wombat burrows, become torpid in cold weather and hibernate in alpine areas for up to 28 weeks over winter, arousing briefly every 2-3 weeks. They have a slow, rolling gait, and can swim well. If threatened they freeze or curl up and eventually seek shelter or bury themselves on the spot. Generally solitary, they have overlapping home ranges of up to 70 ha. In the breeding season up to 10 males follow a receptive female in single file (sometimes for several weeks) until she stops and grasps a tree with her forelimbs. The males dig trenches next to her, but the strongest dislodges the others and lifts her up to mate. Pregnant females dig a nursery burrow 1-1.5 m long. **Development** Echidnas may live to 50 years and mate from June to September. Females develop a temporary abdominal pouch in the breeding season, and about 2 weeks after mating curl up and lay a single egg, about 15 mm long with a leathery skin, directly into the pouch. It hatches after 10 days and the newborn suckles from 2 milk patches next to the pouch, staying there until it begins to grow spines at 6-9 weeks. Still blind, it is left in the nursery burrow (with the entrance plugged) while the mother forages. She returns every 3-10 days and suckles it for another 4-5 months. **Diet** Termites, ants, worms, and other invertebrates, dug up with the forefeet, gathered and crushed with the tongue. **Habitat** Most habitats from forests to deserts, to about 1400 m, except farmlands, upland rainforests and fern gullies. **Traces** Conical diggings. Scats are long cylinders up to about 2 cm across and 5 cm long, light to dark brown, containing insect fragments. **Status** Secure. **Length** 300-450 mm. **Weight** 2-7 kg. Males are larger.

Platypus

Ornithorhynchus anatinus

A streamlined, egg-laying aquatic mammal with webbed feet and a flattened, paddle-like tail. It lacks external ears, but has a rubbery, duck-shaped bill lined with receptors able to pick up tiny electrical signals emitted by aquatic invertebrates. Its fur is soft, dense and water-repellent, dark-brown above, pale cream and sometimes reddish below. The feet have long, sharp claws. Males have a sharp, hollow, spur about 12 mm long on the ankles of their hindlegs, connected to a venom gland in the groin, probably used against other males in the breeding season. Females lose the spur before maturity. **Behaviour** Active from dusk to early morning, and by day in cold weather, Platypuses are generally solitary, living in home ranges of up to 3.5 km along rivers. Female home ranges overlap, while those of males are exclusive. They have a waddling walk supported by the knuckles of the forelimbs, and swim with a rolling dive, closing their eyes, nostrils and ears under water. Aquatic animals are caught or sifted from the river bed by the bill, stored in cheek pouches and ground between horny ridges after surfacing. Individuals use several burrows about 2 m long, and 10-12 cm wide, with entrances submerged or hidden under a log. Breeding females dig a nesting burrow above water level, up to 20 m long, ending in a grass-lined nest chamber. In cold climates they hibernate from May to September. **Development** Sexually mature at 2 years, they mate in the water from August to October. Females usually lay 2 eggs about 17 mm long with soft leathery skins, and curl around them until they hatch about 10 days later. Newborn feed for 3-4 months on milk suckled from ducts on the mother's belly and may be left in the nest for up to 36 hours while she forages. They are weaned at 17 weeks and live to 11 years or more. **Diet** Insects, molluscs, worms, shrimps, trout eggs and small vertebrates. **Habitat** Streams and lakes from the highlands to coastal waterways, in forests and rainforests to 1400 m. **Traces** Mud slides and surface bubbles. Scats are greyish-brown pellets of mostly fine silt particles, about 5 mm across and 1 cm long, deposited around burrow entrances. **Status** Vulnerable; threatened by pollution, and habitat destruction. **Length** 380-580 mm. **Weight** 660-2600 g. Males are larger than females.

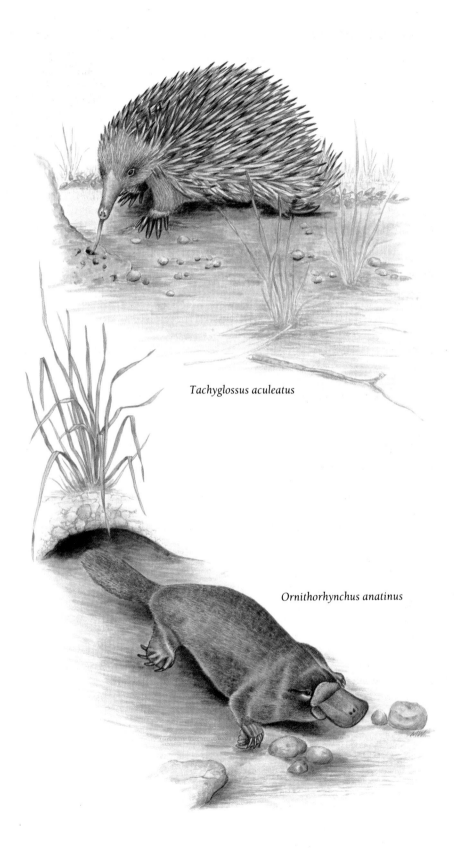

Tachyglossus aculeatus

Ornithorhynchus anatinus

Marsupial Mole

Notoryctes typhlops

This elusive, fascinating animal closely resembles the eutherian Golden Mole of Africa. Adapted to an underground existence, the Marsupial Mole is blind with tiny vestigial eyes, and lacks external ears, having only small holes covered by dense hair. A horny shield protects the nostrils, while the tail is reduced to a leathery stub. The forefeet comprise essentially 2 spade-like shovelling claws, and the hindfeet are clawless. The body is covered with long, silky, golden-brown fur. **Behaviour** Marsupial Moles live mostly underground, only occasionally venturing to the surface, usually after rain. They are extensive burrowers, digging with the flattened claws of the forefeet, pushing the soil out with the hindfeet and tail while they progress forward. Burrows are 10-20 cm below ground with vertical shafts more than 2 m deep linking horizontal tunnels which collapse frequently. In sandy desert soils they seem to swim through the sand as the tunnel fills in behind them. They sleep below ground and may feed on the surface where they pull themselves along in a rapid shuffle, leaving parallel furrows behind and changing direction frequently. Marsupial Moles make sharp squeaking sounds if disturbed and are thought to be solitary. **Development** Males lack a visible scrotum, the testes are located between the skin and abdominal wall. Females have a deep, rear-opening pouch completely covering 2 teats. Little is known about their reproduction and development. **Diet** Ants, termites, beetles, larvae and seeds. **Habitat** Sand dunes and sandy soils of river flats in desert areas. **Status** Probably secure. **Traces** Tracks of 3 parallel furrows in the sand, leading to a small hole. **Head-body** 120-160 mm. **Tail** 20-26 mm. **Weight** 40-70 g.

Numbat

Myrmecobius fasciatus

The Numbat is the only marsupial adapted to feeding on termites. Like the Echidna it has poorly-developed teeth and a long, sticky, cylindrical tongue that flicks rapidly in and out of the long snout to collect termites. The fur is reddish-brown above becoming darker on the rump which has a number of white transverse stripes. The belly is pale-grey to white. A dark stripe runs across the eye from ear to mouth. It has a white patch below the eyes and white eyebrows. The ears are large, the tail bushy and flecked with brown and white hairs, the forelimbs have sharp claws. **Behaviour** Active by day, Numbats sleep in nests of shredded bark, leaves or other soft plant material carried in the mouth and placed in hollow logs or in a spherical nest chamber about 250 mm diameter at the end of a shallow, sloping burrow 1-2 m long. Some burrows are used as bolt holes and others for overnight shelter and rearing young. Numbats are solitary with home ranges of 25-50 ha, although males roam over large areas in the breeding season searching for females. They have a brisk quadrupedal gait and frequently sniff the air while standing on the hindlegs. Numbats locate termites in logs and shallow galleries by scent, digging into the runways leading from the nest. They cannot breach hard termite mounds. **Development** Females are sexually mature at about 11 months, males at 2 years. They breed from January to March, and up to 4 young are born some 14 days after mating. Newborn attach to the 4 exposed teats on the mother's abdomen, clinging to hairs surrounding them and being dragged around until furred in late July. They are then left in the nest while the mother forages until they become independent in November. Juveniles disperse 15 km or more from their maternal home range. **Diet** Termites, consuming 15-20,000 per day. **Habitat** Eucalypt forests dominated by Wandoo or Jarrah. **Status** Endangered; threatened by Fox and Cat predation and land clearing. **Traces** Small conical scratchings around termite mounds. Scats are smooth dark cylinders with rounded ends, to 1 cm across and 1-2 cm long, deposited on fallen logs and at feeding sites. **Head-body** 200-275 mm. **Tail** 160-210 mm. **Weight** 280-715 g.

Notoryctes typhlops

Myrmecobius fasciatus

Northern Quoll

Dasyurus hallucatus

The Northern Quoll is a carnivorous marsupial the size of a large rat. It is the smallest quoll with brownish-grey to brown fur with white spots on the back, but not on the tail, and cream to white belly fur. The head is long and pointed with large bulging eyes and large pointed ears. The hindfeet have 5 toes with furrowed pads; the first toe lacks a claw. **Behaviour** Active mainly at night, Northern Quolls are good climbers although most of their time is spent on the ground. They sleep in dens in hollow tree trunks, hollow logs, crevices and holes in termite mounds. They are very aggressive and emit sharp screeches if threatened. Males and females maintain home ranges, and during the breeding season males are under great stress, fighting of other males in defence of an area that includes a number of resident breeding females. Most juvenile males and some young females leave the mother's home range at 6-8 months old. **Development** Sexually mature at 10-11 months, females may live for 2-3 years although all adult males die from stress-related illnesses soon after mating. They breed in late June, giving birth to up to 8 young in July. Females have no true pouch although ridges of skin develop on either side of their 6-8 teats during the breeding season. The young remain firmly attached to the teats for the first 8-10 weeks, when they are still blind but well-furred. They are then left in the den while the mother forages, and are weaned at about 5 months. **Diet** Small mammals, reptiles, insects, larvae and soft fruits. **Habitat** Favours rocky areas in open forests, savanna and woodland. **Status** Secure. **Traces** Scats are about 1 cm across and 3 cm long, usually twisted and pointed at one end, containing fragments of insects, bones, fur and feathers, deposited on conspicuous high places on rock piles or boulders and at den entrances. **Head-body** 125-310 mm. **Tail** 125-310 mm. **Weight** 300-950 g. Males are larger than females.

Spotted-tailed Quoll

Dasyurus maculatus

A ferocious, Cat-sized marsupial, the Spotted-tailed Quoll is the largest marsupial carnivore on the mainland. It has a powerful body with rich reddish-brown to olive-brown or chocolate fur, with white spots of various sizes on the back and tail, and pale creamy-yellow belly fur. A good climber, it has a long tail for balance, sharp curved claws, ridged pads on the feet, and an opposable clawless thumb on the hindfoot for gripping branches. The face is relatively short with a squat, blunt muzzle. **Behaviour** Spotted-tailed Quolls are active at night, although on cool winter days they sometimes hunt and bask in the sun. Although mainly terrestrial, they are agile climbers and run with a bounding gait, otherwise their movements are slow and deliberate, sniffing regularly for signs of food. They climb trees to spot and pounce on prey, hunting and scavenging within a large home range, often covering several kilometres in one night. Sleeping birds are knocked from branches and caught as they fall. Food is manipulated with the forepaws, and larger prey is killed by biting the back of the neck and head. They sleep in dens in hollow trees, hollow logs, caves, rock crevices or abandoned burrows. Dens are shared after mating by family groups, and defended aggressively by both sexes. Males fight for dominance during the mating season, uttering growls and staccato cries during courtship. Females make soft `chh-chh-chh' calls to their young, and males sometimes bring food to the suckling mother. **Development** Sexually mature at one year, they breed from April to July, and copulation may last 8 hours. Females have a shallow, rear-opening pouch partially covering 6 teats. Up to 6 young are born some 21 days after mating and attach to the mother's teats for about 7 weeks. They are then left in the den while the mother forages, venturing out at about 14 weeks and becoming independent at about 18 weeks. **Diet** An opportunistic hunter and scavenger of birds, reptiles, insects and small to medium-sized mammals, particularly Rabbits. **Habitat** Wet and dry sclerophyll forests, rainforests, woodlands, coastal heaths. **Traces** Scats are often left in conspicuous places. They are 1-2 cm across and up to about 6 cm long, often twisted and pointed, dark to pale brown, containing fragments of bone, feathers, fur, reptile scales or insect remains. **Status** Vulnerable; sparsely distributed; threatened by land clearing, logging, poisoned baits and competition from Cats and Foxes. **Head-body** 350-760 mm. **Tail** 340-550 mm. **Weight** 2-7 kg. Males are larger than females.

Dasyurus hallucatus

Dasyurus maculatus

Eastern Quoll

Dasyurus viverrinus

The size of a small Cat, this carnivorous marsupial is a medium to slender build with
dense soft fur. Two distinct colour phases exist, often in the same litter: either
black with a brown belly or fawn with a white belly; both have white spots on the
back but not on the tail. They have large rounded ears, relatively short legs and
only 4 toes on the hindfeet. **Behaviour** Active mainly at night, they hunt alone in
open grasslands, among the undergrowth and among the lower branches of trees,
climbing well and often standing erect on their hindlegs sniffing the air. They sleep in grass-
lined dens, often with several chambers, in short burrows, hollow logs, rock piles or dense vegetation.
Usually solitary, they have overlapping home ranges, utilising and occasionally sharing a number of dens, particularly during the breeding season when social interactions increase and fighting often occurs between males. Males
change dens frequently but do not share with other males. They utter a guttural growl when alarmed.
Development Sexually mature at one year, Eastern Quolls breed from May to June. Females have no true pouch
although ridges of skin develop on either side of the 5-8 teats during the breeding season. More than 8 young are
usually born 20-24 days after mating, but only those able to attach to a teat survive. A second litter may be produced if the first is lost early in lactation. Newborn are only about 6 mm long, attach firmly to the mother's teats,
and are dragged around for 6-8 weeks. They are then left in the den or are carried on her back if she changes dens,
until weaned at about 16 weeks, becoming independent at 20-29 weeks. **Diet** Small mammals including mice,
bandicoots, Rabbits, reptiles, ground-nesting birds, large insects and their larvae, fruits, seeds and grasses. They
also scavenge the carcasses of large animals. **Habitat** Wet and dry sclerophyll forests, heath and scrubland.
Status Vulnerable; sparsely distributed in Tas.; possibly extinct on the mainland. **Traces** Scats are 1-2 cm across
and up to about 6 cm long, twisted, containing bones, fur and feathers, or insect remains. **Head-body** 280-450 mm.
Tail 170-280 mm. **Weight** 600-2000 g. Males are usually larger than females.

Tasmanian Devil

Sarcophilus harrisii

Largest of the carnivorous marsupials, the Tasmanian Devil is powerfully built with
small eyes set in a short, broad head with strong jaws and well-developed teeth. The
fur is black, usually with white patches on the neck and rump. The muzzle and
small rounded ears are sparsely-haired, and they blush deep red if stressed. The
limbs are short with strong claws. Fat is stored in the tail which becomes carrot-
shaped. **Behaviour** Active mainly at night, they sleep in grass-lined dens in burrows up to 15 m long, with one or more entrances 20-30 cm diameter, sometimes shared by 2 or
more animals. They also shelter in hollow logs, caves, rock piles and wombat burrows, and males make
use of several dens. Devils are generally solitary with large overlapping home ranges of some 8-20 sq km. They are
shy, opportunistic carnivores and inept killers, feeding mainly on carcasses, following well-defined trails to food
sources, and gathering in groups to feed on large animals where they fight noisily over the remains. Devils establish dominance hierarchies and engage in ritualised aggression, standing on their hind legs and locking jaws,
uttering loud growls, yells and screams. They move with an awkward slow lope and a rocking run, can climb trees,
and may travel 8 km in a night. **Development** Sexually mature at 2 years old, Devils live to about 6 years. They
breed in March, and mate repeatedly over a 10 day period, with a dominant male guarding a female. Usually 2-3
young are born 21 days after mating. Each attaches to one of the 4 teats in the mother's shallow, backward-opening
pouch, where they remain until fully-furred at 13-16 weeks. The young are then left in the den while the mother forages, and are weaned at 28-30 weeks, becoming independent at 40 weeks. **Diet** Carrion, including bones, supplemented by large insects, birds and other small animals. **Habitat** All major habitats, preferring sclerophyll forests,
scrub and woodland. **Status** Probably secure; protected. **Traces** Scats are grey, about 2 cm across and 3-6 cm long,
pointed and twisted with fur at one end, full of bone and fur fragments, often deposited on walking tracks.
Head-body 500-710 mm. **Tail** 240-310 mm. **Weight** 7-10 kg. Males are larger than females.

Dasyurus viverrinus

Sarcophilus harrisii

Kowari

Dasyuroides byrnei

A rat-size carnivorous marsupial, the Kowari is light grey-brown to sandy-brown above, usually with a darker stripe along the forehead, and greyish-white below. The terminal half of the tail has a brush of dark-brown hairs. The pointed head has large eyes and thin, sparsely-haired ears. The limbs are quite long with 4 toes on the hindfeet. **Behaviour** Active mainly at night, Kowaris are ground-dwellers, running with a bounding gait, and sitting up on their hindlegs if disturbed. They sometimes bask in the sun on winter days, and become torpid for short periods when food is scarce. They dig burrows for daytime shelter, or modify those of other mammals such as the Bilby or some rodents, and sleep in a nest lined with leaves and other vegetable matter. Some burrows have a number of entrances, and individuals use several burrows. Generally solitary, they occupy overlapping home ranges of several sq km, scent-marking the boundaries with urine, scats and secretions from a chest gland. Vocalisations include a loud defensive staccato chattering and a threatening hiss accompanied by vigorous tail movements. **Development** Females first breed in their second year, mating from May to December, and copulating for several hours over a 3-day period. They may produce 2 litters of up to 6 young per year, born 30-35 days after mating. A shallow pouch develops from skin folds before birth, leaving the mother's 6 teats exposed. Newborn are about 3 mm long and attach firmly to the teats, where they are partially enclosed in the pouch until about 30 days old. They then hang below the mother, and are dragged around until detaching from the teats some 3 weeks later. The young are then left in the nest or cling to the mother's back while she hunts, until they are weaned at about 4 months. **Diet** Insects, small vertebrates and carrion. They do not need to drink if the food is moist. **Habitat** Stony deserts with sparse vegetation. **Status** Endangered; threatened by grazing and Fox predation. **Traces** Scats are about 5 mm across and up to 4 cm long, twisted and pointed at one end, strong-smelling, left as markers near burrows and on rocks. **Head-body** 135-180 mm. **Tail** 110-140 mm. **Weight** 70-140 g. Males are larger than females.

Mulgara

Dasycercus cristicauda

A small, robust, carnivorous marsupial of the central Australian deserts, the Mulgara has fine soft fur, light sandy-brown with a dark-grey base on the back, and greyish-white belly fur. The short tail has a fattened, reddish base and a striking crest of dark-brown hairs along the terminal half. The conical head has large eyes and thin, sparsely-haired ears. The hindfeet have 5 toes with furrowed pads.
Behaviour Active mainly at night, Mulgaras sleep in grass-lined nests in complex burrow systems, often with several entrances about 25 mm across, numerous vertical shafts and deep, branching side tunnels. Burrows are dug in the flats between sand dunes or on the slopes of high dunes. Individuals use several burrows within their home range and make well-defined paths from the burrow entrance to a nearby bush where piles of scats are deposited. Mulgaras are solitary, socialising briefly during the breeding season, and may be seen basking in the sun on cold days. They run with a bounding gait and sit upright on their hind legs if disturbed. Fast efficient killers, they skin their prey neatly, leaving the inverted skin behind.
Development Sexually mature at 10-11 months, Mulgaras probably continue growing throughout their lives, living to 7 years or more. They breed from May to July. Females develop a shallow pouch on either side of their 6 teats during the breeding season, and give birth to up to 6 young 35-42 days after mating. Newborn attach firmly to the teats and are dragged around for 55-60 days. They are then left in the nest until weaned at 3-4 months. **Diet** Large insects and small vertebrates. They can survive without drinking. **Habitat** Arid, sandy, inland deserts, gibber plains and spinifex grasslands. **Status** Endangered; threatened by grazing stock and predation by Cats. **Traces** Scats are up to 5 mm across and 2 cm long, strong-smelling, twisted at one end, containing bone, fur and insect fragments, and left as markers near burrow entrances and on rocks. **Head-body** 125-220 mm. **Tail** 70-130 mm. **Weight** 60-170 g. Males are larger than females.

Dasyuroides byrnei

Dasycercus cristicauda

Red-tailed Phascogale

Phascogale calura

A small, predominantly arboreal carnivorous marsupial with a long tail, rufous-brown at the base and black below, with a black, bushy tip. The body fur is ash-grey above and cream to white below. It has a pointed face, bulging eyes and large, thin, crinkled ears. The forefeet have 5 long, clawed toes, the hindfeet have 4 long, clawed toes and a small, clawless, opposable inner toe. **Behaviour** Predominantly nocturnal, they sometimes emerge during the day, and sleep in cup-shaped nests of leaves and bark built in hollow logs and tree hollows. They hunt extensively on the ground, moving with jerky bounds or walking carefully, stalking their prey. They are skilful climbers and can leap 2 m between trees. In the breeding season both sexes secrete a musky substance from their anal glands, and the chest fur of males becomes stained with secretions from a chest gland, thought to be important in maintaining dominance hierarchies. Before giving birth pregnant females force the males to disperse, and all the males die within a few weeks from stress-related illnesses, probably induced by strenuous competition with other males during courtship and mating. **Development** They are sexually mature at about 9 months, with a life expectancy of up to 3 years for females and 11.5 months for males. They mate in July, and up to 13 young are born 28-30 days late. Only those able to attach to the mother's 8 teats survive. Females have no true pouch although ridges of skin develop on either side of the teats in the breeding season. Young are dragged around until they relinquish the teat, and are left in the nest until weaned at 4-5 months. **Diet** Insects, spiders, small birds, rodents, reptiles and possibly carrion. They can survive without drinking. **Habitat** Dry, mature eucalypt forests and shrublands with an annual rainfall of 300-600 mm. **Traces** Scats are 1-3 mm across and about 1 cm long, grey to yellow or brown, comprising insect fragments or narrow twists of fur or feathers. **Status** Endangered; sparsely distributed; threatened by land clearing, logging, bushfires and predation by Cats and Foxes. **Head-body** 90-125 mm. **Tail** 120-145 mm. **Weight** 38-68 g. Males are larger than females.

Brush-tailed Phascogale

Phascogale tapoatafa

A semi-arboreal marsupial with steel-grey fur flecked with black above and pale cream below. The non-prehensile tail has a bushy tip with black hairs up to 40 mm long. The forefeet have 5 long, thin, clawed toes, while the hindfeet have 4 long toes with long, sharp claws, very flexible joints, and an opposing small, clawless first toe, enabling it to grasp branches. The head is long and pointed with large bulging eyes and long ears. **Behaviour** Active at night, they are fast, agile climbers, running below branches, leaping between trees and rapping their feet on the trunk if threatened. They bite off the bark and extract insects with their long fingers. By day they sleep in nests on the ground or in bird nests, using up to 40 different sites annually, often changing daily. Nursery nests are built in large tree hollows with an entrance 25-40 mm across, lined with leaves, shredded bark, feathers and fur. They are generally solitary, although pairs may share nests in the breeding season. Females have home ranges of 20-70 ha, sometimes shared with their female offspring. Juvenile males disperse and establish overlapping home ranges of more than 100 ha. In the breeding season males travel long distances searching for females, and their chests become stained with yellow secretions. All males die a few weeks after mating due to stress-related illnesses. **Development** They are sexually mature at about 8 months, and females may live to 3 years. Mating occurs in May and June in tree hollows, and copulation can last several hours. Breeding females develop a shallow abdominal pouch from enlarged ridges of skin around the teats. More than 8 young may be produced some 30 days after mating, although only those able to attach to the mother's 8 teats survive. The young are carried around until they detach from the teats at about 7 weeks, when they are left in the nest while the mother forages. They are gradually weaned between 14 and 25 weeks. **Diet** Insects, spiders, centipedes, small vertebrates and nectar from eucalypt flowers. **Habitat** Wet and dry open eucalypt forests and woodlands, preferring ridges and rocky slopes to 1500 m. **Traces** Scats are deposited around dens, on tree branches and logs. They are about 5 mm across and up to 4 cm long, pale yellow to blackish-brown, full of insect fragments or twisted with feathers and fur. **Status** Vulnerable; sparsely distributed; threatened by land clearing, logging and predation by Cats and Foxes. **Head-body** 148-260 mm. **Tail** 160-235 mm. **Weight** 105-310 g. Males are larger than females.

Phascogale calura

Phascogale tapoatafa

Northern Dibbler

Parantechinus bilarni

A mouse-size carnivorous marsupial, the Northern Dibbler has flecked greyish-brown fur above and pale grey belly fur with sandy patches behind its large, thin, crinkled ears. The tail is long and slender, sparsely-haired with visible scales. The head is long with large bulging eyes and a pointed muzzle with little fur on the sides. The feet have furrowed pads to help them grip when climbing. **Behaviour** Northern Dibblers are mainly active at night, although in the winter they are often seen basking in the sun. They are agile climbers, although most of the time is spent on the ground foraging for insects. They sleep during the day in rock crevices, moving to humid vine thickets in the dry season in search of food. Males are more mobile than females, and the majority of juveniles leave the maternal home range and disperse to a new area. **Development** The Northern Dibbler becomes sexually mature at 12 months. Mortality rates are high, and only about one quarter live to see a second breeding season. They breed from late June to early July, usually producing 4-5 young about 38 days later. Newborn attach firmly to the 6 teats on the mother's belly. Females have no true pouch and the young hang from their mother's teats as she moves around. After detaching from the teats they are left in the nest while she forages, and are weaned at 4-5 months. **Diet** Insects, larvae and small invertebrates. **Habitat** Rugged sandstone escarpments with open eucalypt forests, vine thickets and closed forests. **Status** Probably secure; common in a limited habitat. **Head-body** 80-115 mm. **Tail** 90-125 mm. **Weight** 12-40 g. Males are slightly larger than females.

Fat-tailed Pseudantechinus

Pseudantechinus macdonnellensis

A small carnivorous marsupial of the arid desert regions of Australia, the Fat-tailed Pseudantechinus derives its name from the swollen base of the tail where deposits of fat are laid down when food is plentiful. Poorly-nourished individuals use these fat reserves and consequently have a relatively thin tail. The fur is greyish-brown above and greyish-white below with light reddish-brown patches behind the ears. The head is long with a black-tipped, pointed muzzle, large eyes and ears. The hindfeet are broad. **Behaviour** The Fat-tailed Pseudantechinus is active mainly at night, although individuals sometimes emerge during the day in winter to sunbathe. The sleep in rocky crevices or in burrows in termite mounds. **Development** Sexual maturity is reached at the age of 10-11 months and both sexes may live long enough to breed twice. Births are timed to coincide with plentiful food supplies. They breed once a year either in June-July in Central Australia and or in August-September in the western part of their range. Females have no true pouch although ridges of skin develop on either side of the 6 teats during the breeding season, and partially enclose the developing young. Up to 6 young are born 45-55 days after mating and attach themselves firmly to the teats, where they remain, being dragged around by the mother until they detach and are able to be left in the nest while she forages. The young are weaned at about 14 weeks. **Diet** Insects and other small invertebrates. **Habitat** Arid rocky hills and desert country. **Status** Probably secure. **Head-body** 95-105 mm. **Tail** 75-85 mm. **Weight** 20-45 g.

Parantechinus bilarni

Pseudantechinus macdonnellensis

Brown Antechinus

Antechinus stuartii

A small carnivorous marsupial, the Brown Antechinus has dark to orange-brown fur above, paler belly fur and a sparsely-haired tail. It has a long head with bulging eyes and large, thin, crinkled ears with a notched margin. The forefeet have 5 strongly-clawed toes. The hindfeet have 4 long, clawed toes and a small, opposing, clawless inner toe. **Behaviour** Active mainly at night, they usually sleep during the day in spherical nests constructed of plant material in a hollow log, crevice or epiphytic fern. Nests are shared, and on cold days they huddle together or bask in the sun, and become torpid for a few hours to conserve energy when food is scarce. They have a home range of about 1 ha and make use of several nests up to 500 m apart, some of which are female only. As the breeding season approaches the scent gland on the chest of males enlarges and they become very agitated and increasingly aggressive, running around between communal nests looking for females to mate with. Females continue to forage in their home ranges, visiting some of the communal nests to find mates. Copulation lasts about 6 hours, and all males die from stress-related illnesses 5-10 days after the 2 week breeding season ends. Juvenile males disperse long distances from their mother's home range, while the females remain close by. **Development** Females may live for up to 3 years and both sexes are sexually mature at about 10 months. Mating occurs in August or September, and all the females in a particular population ovulate within a few days of one another. They copulate with several different males over a 2 week period, storing the sperm and using it to fertilise their ova at the end of this period. Between 6 and 10 young are born 25-31 days later. Females have no true pouch, although large ridges of skin develop on either side of their 6-10 teats before birth. The young remain firmly attached to the teats and are dragged around by the mother for 4-6 weeks. They are then left in the nest while the mother forages until weaned at about 3 months. **Diet** Cockroaches, beetles, spiders and other small invertebrates gleaned from the forest floor or fissures in tree bark. Flowers and fruit are sometimes eaten. **Habitat** Rainforests and sclerophyll forests, preferring wetter habitats with dense undergrowth and deep leaf litter. **Traces** Scats are light to dark brown, about 2 mm across and up to 15 mm long, friable and packed with insect remains. **Status** Secure. **Head-body** 77-140 mm. **Tail** 65-110 mm. **Weight** 17-71 g. Males are larger than females.

Yellow-footed Antechinus

Antechinus flavipes

One of the more colourful antechinuses, this mouse-size carnivorous marsupial has a slate-grey head grading to orange-brown on the sides, belly, rump and feet, white patches on the throat and belly, a pale ring around the eye and a black tail tip. Northern animals are more brightly coloured. The head is long and pointed with a black muzzle tip, bulging eyes and thin, crinkled ears. The forefeet have 5 long, well-clawed toes, the hindfeet are very broad with 4 clawed toes and a small, opposing, clawed inner toe used to grip branches. **Behaviour** Active mainly at night, they are rarely seen during daylight hours, sleeping in a roughly constructed nest lined with leaves and other vegetation in hollow logs, rocky crevices, caves or buildings. They move quickly and erratically with short bounds and can run upside-down along branches, gripping with their broad feet, uttering high-pitched squeaks if threatened. They bulldoze through the leaf litter and pounce on their prey, killing quickly and efficiently with bites to the head and neck, leaving the skin of small mammals turned inside-out. **Development** Sexually mature at 10-11 months, they have a short mating season from July to September, depending on the climate, and copulation may last for 12 hours. Some females survive to breed the following year, but all males die from stress-related illnesses soon after mating. Up to 14 young are born 23-26 days later, although the number raised depends on the number of teats, which varies from 8-14. Females have no true pouch, although ridges of skin develop on either side of the teats 2 weeks before birth. The young attach firmly to the nipples and are dragged around for about 36 days. They are then left in the nest or ride on the mother's back while she forages, and are weaned at 3-4 months. **Diet** Insects and other invertebrates, small vertebrates, flowers and nectar. **Habitat** Tropical rainforests to cool wet and dry sclerophyll forests and dry mulga woodlands, from sea level to 1000 m. **Traces** Scats are similar to the Brown Antechinus, although some may contain twists of fur or feathers. **Status** Probably secure; vulnerable to loss of old growth forests and lack of suitable tree hollows. **Head-body** 85-165 mm. **Tail** 65-155 mm. **Weight** 21-80 g. Males are larger than females.

28

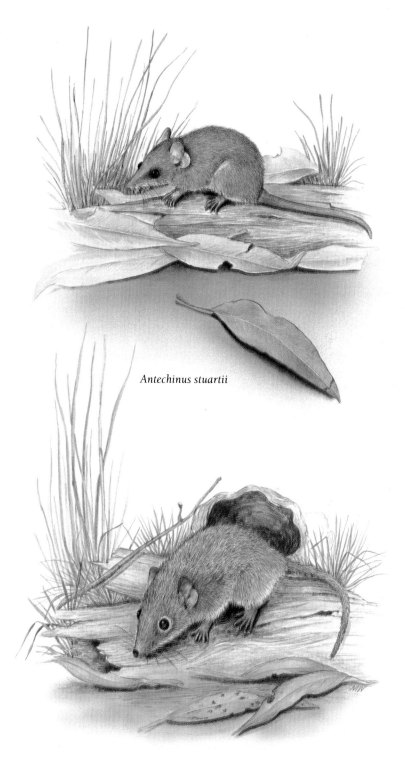

Antechinus stuartii

Antechinus flavipes

Common Dunnart

Sminthopsis murina

Despite its name, this small insectivorous marsupial is not common in most of its range, although it is capable of rapid population growth in good years. It is slate grey above and white below with a long, pointed head with bulging eyes, large ears and a slender muzzle. The hindfeet are less than 3 mm wide with a very small first toe. The tail is slender, sparsely-haired with visible scales. **Behaviour** Common Dunnarts are active mainly at night, and sleep in cup-shaped nests, 70-100 mm wide, of dried grass and leaves constructed in hollow logs, grassy tussocks, natural crevices or grass-trees. In cold weather they become torpid, lowering their body temperature to conserve energy. Males become very aggressive during the breeding season, often fighting over females who attract them by a repetitive chit-chit-chit call. Females may survive to breed a second time, but most males probably die soon after the breeding season. **Development** Sexual maturity is reached at about 6 months, and the breeding season extends from early September to late March. Females mate soon after weaning their first litter, and most females probably produce 2 litters of 8-10 young each breeding season. Young are born only 12.5 days after mating, and attach firmly to the mother's 8-10 teats, completely enclosed in a well-developed circular pouch with a central opening. They develop rapidly, vacating the pouch at about 34 days, and are then left in the nest while the mother forages. They are weaned at 60-65 days and reach adult size by about 5 months. The pouch regresses after weaning. **Diet** Spiders, beetles, caterpillars, cockroaches and other invertebrates. **Habitat** Open forests and woodlands, mallee and heath, to an altitude of 400 m, with an annual rainfall of 250-850 mm. Maximum population densities are reached in areas regenerating after fire. **Traces** Scats are deposited in large numbers near nest sites. They are small, twisted, about 2-4 mm across and up to 15 mm long, friable, containing fine insect fragments. **Status** Probably secure; widespread with patchy distribution and isolated populations. **Head-body** 60-105 mm. **Tail** 68-100 mm. **Weight** 10-28 g. Males are larger than females.

Dusky Antechinus

Antechinus swainsonii

The Dusky Antechinus is a stocky, mouse-size carnivorous marsupial with soft, dense fur, deep chocolate-brown to blackish-brown above and pale-grey below. The head has a long pointed muzzle, small eyes and ears. The broad hindfeet have 4 long, clawed toes and a small, clawless, opposing first toe for gripping branches. The forefeet have 5 toes with long, curved claws for digging. **Behaviour** Active both day and night, they sleep in shallow burrows often dug into creek banks, under logs or in cavities in logs or stumps. Tunnels are less than 1 m long and terminate in a spherical, leaf or grass-lined nesting chamber about 10 cm across. They are very active and fast-moving with short, jerky bounds, and may be seen climbing among the lower limbs of trees, searching among leaf litter or digging for food. In alpine areas they forage in tunnels beneath the snow. They maintain a home range, and females move their young between nests if disturbed. Males are solitary except during the mating season when they become very aggressive towards other males and smear objects with secretions from their chest gland. Copulation is violent and may last 6 hours. Less than half of the females survive to the next breeding season, but all males die of stress-related illnesses within 3 weeks of mating. Juvenile males disperse abruptly from the maternal home range, while young females remain close by. **Development** Sexually mature at about 11 months, mating is highly synchronised in each population and takes place from June to August, or September in alpine areas. All females ovulate within 10 days of each other. Up to 10 young are born 28-35 days after mating, but only those able to attach to the mother's 6-8 teats survive. Females have no true pouch; ridges of skin enlarge around the teats before birth, forming a shallow pouch divided by a central ridge. The young remain firmly attached to the nipples and are dragged around until they are 7-8 weeks old. They are then left in the nest while the mother forages, venturing out at about 10 weeks, often carried on her back until they are independent at about 13 weeks. **Diet** Small vertebrates, worms, beetles, centipedes, spiders, and other invertebrates. **Habitat** Wet sclerophyll forests and woodlands with a dense understorey, rainforests, wet heaths and alpine heaths to 1800 m. **Traces** Scats are light to dark brown, 2-7 mm across and up to 3 cm long, twisted with fur or feathers, or packed with insect remains. **Status** Secure; widespread but rarely abundant. **Head-body** 90-190 mm. **Tail** 70-130 mm. **Weight** 35-180 g. Males are larger than females.

Sminthopsis murina

Antechinus swainsonii

White-footed Dunnart

Sminthopsis leucopus

A slightly-built, mouse-size carnivorous marsupial, the White-footed Dunnart has soft, light-grey fur on its back, becoming darker on the rump and pale-grey to white belly fur. It has a long pointed muzzle, large bulging eyes, large rounded ears, a scaly tail with sparse, coarse hairs and very narrow hindfeet with furrowed pads to help it grip when climbing. **Behaviour** Active mainly at night, White-footed Dunnarts are very fast on the ground and good climbers. They sleep in nests lined with roughly-shredded bark in tree hollows, rotting logs, wood piles, under bark sheets and in underground burrows. Generally solitary, they have small overlapping home ranges of about 1 ha, and travel up to 1.5 km looking for food. Males do not survive to breed a second year and seem to disperse within one month of the young becoming independent. **Development** Mating occurs in July and August, with births in late August and September, and most individuals have only one short breeding season in their lives. Up to 10 young about 3 mm long are born and attach firmly to the mother's 8-10 teats, completely enclosed in a circular pouch with a central opening, remaining there for about 8 weeks. **Diet** A range of ground-dwelling invertebrates including insects and their larvae, small reptiles and possibly small mammals. **Habitat** Woodlands and open forests, wet heath, sedgeland, tussock grassland and coastal scrub, from sea level to 400 m, with an annual rainfall of around 600-1000 mm. **Traces** Scats are small, twisted, about 2-3 mm across and up to 15 mm long, very friable and full of insect fragments, deposited in small piles in the nest. **Status** Probably secure, but endangered in NSW; sparsely distributed. **Head-body** 65-120 mm. **Tail** 45-105 mm. **Weight** 20-35 g. Males are larger than females.

Red-cheeked Dunnart

Sminthopsis virginiae

A small carnivorous marsupial of northern Australia and New Guinea, the Red-cheeked Dunnart has short, spiky fur, blackish-brown flecked with white above, white, yellow or rufous below, with reddish cheeks and a distinct blackish stripe down the forehead. The tail is narrow, sparsely haired and scaly. The hindfeet are narrow with 4 long toes and a small first digit. The head is long and pointed with large bulging eyes and large rounded ears. **Behaviour** Red-cheeked Dunnarts are active mainly at night and sleep during the day under logs and dense vegetation. Shortly before giving birth pregnant females build a shallow, saucer-shaped nest of shredded leaves and grass hidden under dense grass or pandanus leaves. They are solitary except during the breeding season. **Development** Red-cheeked Dunnarts become sexually mature at about 7 months and continue to grow throughout their lives. They are capable of breeding throughout the year, although this has not been verified in the wild. Females with suckling young have been found in March and July-November. Females may produce 2 litters per season of up to 8 young, born about 15 days after mating. Newborn attach firmly to the mother's 8 teats and are fully-enclosed in a well-developed circular pouch with a central opening. When they emerge from the pouch the young are left in the nest while the mother forages for food. They are weaned at 65-70 days. **Diet** A range of small invertebrates including insects and spiders, and possibly small vertebrates. **Habitat** Savanna woodlands. **Status** Probably secure; sparsely distributed. **Traces** Scats are thin, twisted, up to 5 mm across and 2 cm long, friable and full of fine insect fragments, deposited around nest sites. **Head-body** 90-135 mm. **Tail** 90-135 mm. **Weight** 18-60 g.

Sminthopsis leucopus

Sminthopsis virginiae

Fat-tailed Dunnart

Sminthopsis crassicaudata

A widespread, mouse-sized, carnivorous marsupial, the Fat-tailed Dunnart is brownish-grey above and light-grey to white below. The fur has a dark base and sandy-
grey tips. It has a pointed head with large bulging eyes and very large ears. Fat
is stored in the short tail, which resembles a small carrot in well-nourished individuals. **Behaviour** Active only at night, they sleep by day in cup-shaped nests of
dried grass, 7-10 cm across, beneath logs, rocky crevices or fissures in the cracked
soil in arid areas. Solid spherical nests are sometimes built. In cold weather they often huddle
together in the nest to keep warm, and may be seen basking in the early morning sun. They become
torpid for a number of hours if food is short, dropping their body temperature to conserve energy and utilising fat
reserves in the tail. They are generally solitary and hunt for invertebrates on the ground, sometimes in open areas.
They have large, drifting home ranges that change according to the food supply. **Development** Sexual maturity is
reached at 5 months, although females do not breed in the year of their birth. Most females live for less than 18
months, while few males live more than 15 months. The breeding season extends from July to February with birth
peaks in August and September, coinciding with the seasonal abundance of food, and 2 litters are usually raised in
a year. The gestation period is very short, and 8-10 young are born only 13 days after mating. They attach firmly to
the 8-10 teats in the mother's well-developed circular pouch with a central opening, detaching at around 43 days
and leaving the pouch permanently at about 60 days. The young are then left in the nest while the mother forages,
and are carried on her back if she moves between nesting sites until they are weaned at about 10 weeks.
Diet Insects, earthworms and other small invertebrates; rarely small vertebrates such as frogs. They can exist without drinking. **Habitat** Moist coastal to arid inland areas with open woodlands, low open shrubland, sparse tussock
grasslands, gibber plains and farmland, from sea level to 400 m. **Traces** Scats are small, twisted, 2-4 mm across and
up to about 15 mm long, friable, packed with insect fragments, deposited in piles near nest sites. **Status** Secure.
Head-body 60-90 mm. **Tail** 40-70 mm. **Weight** 10-20 g. Males are larger than females.

White-tailed Dunnart

Sminthopsis granulipes

A small, delicate, carnivorous marsupial, the White-tailed Dunnart has long, soft fur
with a blue-grey base and dark-brown tips on the back, giving it an overall light-fawn
to grey colour. The tail is white with a thin dark-brown stripe along the upper
surface. The head is pointed with a narrow muzzle, large bulging eyes and large
ears with notched margins. It has white paws and rasp-like granulations on the
soles of the forefeet and hindfeet. **Behaviour** Although common in its habitat, the
White-tailed Dunnart has been little studied. It is known to be active at night, when it hunts for
insects. Dunnarts have a high metabolic rate and when food is short they fall into a state of torpor, lowering their metabolic rate to conserve energy. **Development** The breeding season is probably between May and July.
Females have a circular pouch with a central opening. Young are probably weaned in September-October.
Diet Insects and their larvae, spiders and centipedes. **Habitat** Low shrubland, sparse mallee with shrubby ground
cover, mostly on sand. **Status** Probably secure. **Head-body** 69-88 mm. **Tail** 56-66 mm. **Weight** 18-37 g.

Sminthopsis crassicaudata

Sminthopsis granulipes

Hairy-footed Dunnart

Sminthopsis hirtipes

A small, mouse-size, carnivorous marsupial of the drier regions, the Hairy-footed Dunnart is yellowish-brown to grey-brown above and light grey to white below. The base of the tail is slightly swollen and becomes fatter in good seasons. The feet are broad and long (16-19 mm) with fat toes with granular soles fringed with long, fine silvery hairs extending beyond the feet. The hairs are thought to help them walk on soft sand. The head is long with a narrow pointed muzzle, large ears and large bulging eyes. **Behaviour** The Hairy-footed Dunnart has been little-studied, partly because of the unsuccessful collecting techniques used in the past. It is active at night, and individuals have been found in deep burrows probably made by hopping mice, and in abandoned bull-ant nests. Dunnarts have a high metabolic rate and when food is scarce they become torpid, lower their metabolic rate to conserve energy and use fat reserves stored in the tail. **Development** Lactating females have been found in February and April, suggesting spring and summer breeding seasons, although it is likely that the breeding season relates to rainfall, with population increases after sufficient rain. Females have 6 teats enclosed in a circular pouch with a central opening. Hairy-footed Dunnarts have a lifespan of at least 3 years in the wild. **Diet** Insects and their larvae, small lizards. **Habitat** Sandy arid to semi-arid low open woodlands, shrublands, heaths and hummock grasslands on plains or sand dunes. **Status** Probably secure. **Head-body** 70-85 mm. **Tail** 70-100 mm. **Weight** 13-20 g.

Stripe-faced Dunnart

Sminthopsis macroura

This small, widespread, carnivorous marsupial is found over vast areas of the arid and semi-arid regions of Australia. The fur is brownish-grey to dark-brown flecked with light grey above, with a prominent dark strip along the forehead, and pale grey to white below. The head is long and pointed with large bulging eyes and large ears. The tail is long, sparsely-haired with a fattened base in well-nourished individuals, and tapers to a point. **Behaviour** Little studied, they are known to be active at night, sheltering from the hot sun during the day under rocks or logs, in dense vegetation, tussock grasses or in cracks in the ground. In cold conditions or when food is short they enter a state of torpor for a few hours, lowering their body temperature to that of the surroundings, conserving energy and using fat stored in the tail. **Development** Sexual maturity is reached at 4-5 months in females and about 9 months in males. They can raise 2 litters per year of 6-8 young in good seasons. Mating takes place from June to November, with most births occurring in July and August and October to January. The young are born only 10-11 days after mating and firmly attach to the 8 teats in the mother's well-developed, centrally-opening, circular pouch. They detach from the teats and leave the pouch at about 40 days and are then left in the nest while the mother forages until they are weaned at about 70 days. **Diet** Insects and other small invertebrates. They can probably survive without drinking. **Habitat** Arid and semi-arid low shrubland, woodland, spinifex and tussock grassland. **Status** Vulnerable; threatened by grazing stock. **Head-body** 70-100 mm. **Tail** 80-110 mm. **Weight** 15-25 g.

Sminthopsis hirtipes

Sminthopsis macroura

Paucident Planigale

Planigale gilesi

A tiny, desert-dwelling carnivorous marsupial, the Paucident Planigale has soft, dense fur, cinnamon-grey with a black base above and olive-buff below. The head is flattened and triangular with small rounded ears and protruding eyes. The tail tapers to the tip, becoming carrot-shaped in good seasons when the base is swollen with stored fat. The limbs are adapted for climbing in soil cracks with short, broad, 5-toed feet with granular pads. It has only 2 premolar teeth (other planigales have 3 premolars). **Behaviour** Active mainly at night, Paucident Planigales are ferocious hunters and efficient killers, climbing among grass and shrubs and slithering through the ground litter searching for insects. They walk with their hindfeet swinging outside the body line, keep low to the ground, and run with a scurrying run gait taking short leaps and bounds. During daylight hours they sleep in nests in hollow logs, under bark, in grass clumps or short burrows, some with a number of side tunnels and sleeping chambers. In winter they share nests for warmth, bask in the sun, and become torpid for short periods when food is scarce. Individuals have shifting home ranges of some 2000 sq m, and males may establish dominance hierarchies. They are very mobile for most of the year, travelling more than 1 km during the night; but during the breeding season females stay in small home ranges and are more sedentary. Vocalisations include an aggressive 'chh-chh' or 'ca-ca', a high-pitched twittering when stressed, and a clicking sound during courtship. **Development** They have an extended breeding season from July to February. Copulation may last more than 2 hours, and females can produce 2 litters per season of 6-8 young, usually born 16 days after mating. Newborn attach firmly to one of the 12 teats in the mother's rear-opening pouch, where they remain for about 37 days. Thereafter they are suckled in the nest until 65-70 days old. They have a lifespan of 5 years, but few live more than 2 years. **Diet** Invertebrates including beetles, spiders, cockroaches and slaters, and occasionally reptiles and small mammals. **Habitat** Arid sandplains, floodplains and creek beds with cracking clay soil with a cover of woodlands, grasslands or sedges. **Traces** Scats are small, twisted, less than 3 mm across, friable and full of insect remains. **Status** Probably secure; rare in Vic.; sparsely distributed with seasonal population fluctuations; vulnerable to habitat disturbance, trampling by stock, and introduced predators. **Head-body** 60-85 mm. **Tail** 55-72 mm. **Weight** 5-16 g. Males are larger than females.

Kultarr

Antechinomys laniger

This mouse-size carnivorous marsupial of the arid and semi-arid regions is fawn-grey to sandy-brown above and white below, with a dark ring around the eye and a darker forehead. The tail is very long and thin with a bushy tip of darker hairs. The head is large with bulging eyes and very large ears. The hind legs are very long with only 4 toes. **Behaviour** Active mainly at night, Kultarrs are terrestrial animals, moving on all-fours, bounding from the hindlegs to the forefeet. They have great manoeuvrability, pivot on their forefeet to escape predators and stand up on their hind legs if disturbed or inquisitive. They shelter under logs, rocks, spinifex and saltbush tussocks, in cracks in the soil, in the burrows of other small animals; or they may dig shallow burrows, concealing the entrance with grass. They are generally solitary, coming together during the mating season. When food is scarce they become torpid to save energy. **Development** Sexually mature at 8 months, Kultarrs breed from July to January, although the timing depends on the geographical location. Females develop a crescent-shaped pouch during the breeding season and may produce more than one litter of 5-8 young per season. The young each attach to one of the mother's 6 or 8 teats, and are partially enclosed in the rear-opening pouch until about 25 mm long at about 30 days old. They are then left in the nest or ride on the mother's back while she forages for food, becoming independent at about 3 months. **Diet** Insects and other small invertebrates. **Habitat** Desert plains, arid and semi-arid grasslands and scrublands. **Status** Probably secure, but endangered in NSW; threatened by pastoral activities. **Head-body** 70-100 mm. **Tail** 100-150 mm. **Weight** 20-40 g. Males are larger than females.

Planigale gilesi

Antechinomys laniger

Narrow-nosed Planigale

Planigale tenuirostris

This tiny carnivorous marsupial derives its name from its slender flattened snout, used to probe into cracks or litter in search of prey. The silky fur has a black base with brown tips giving the back a russet-brown appearance flecked with black, and a faint dark stripe down the forehead. The belly fur is olive-buff to white. The ears are large with a number of folds. It has a short, thin tail and the hind legs have great flexibility allowing them to climb easily and investigate narrow crevices. **Behaviour** Active mainly at night, Narrow-nosed Planigales spend much of their time scurrying around in cracks in the ground, climbing the vertical sides, often standing upright sniffing the air. They are ferocious hunters, killing insects as large as themselves and holding food with their forepaws. In winter they huddle together in nests of dried grass and bask in the sun, becoming torpid for short periods if food is scarce. They have shifting home ranges and may cover more than 500 m overnight foraging for food. Males travel widely during the breeding season, probably looking for females to mate with, and scent-marking areas by rubbing with their chest gland. They fight frequently, make short "tsst, tsst" calls to attract females, and may establish dominance hierarchies giving the largest individuals mating preferences. Vocalisations are often loud and include an aggressive "chh-chh-chh", a defensive "ca-ca-ca" and high-pitched twittering when stressed. **Development** The breeding season extends from early August to January, and females can produce 2 litters of 6-8 young per season. Young are born 19 days after mating, are 3 mm long and attach firmly to the 10-12 teats in the mother's rear-opening pouch. They detach from the teats at about 40 days and are left in the nest while the mother forages for food. Their eyes open at about 51 days and they are suckled for about 95 days. They grow throughout their lives and may live for 2-3 years. **Diet** Insects, spiders, and other arthropods. They do not need to drink. **Habitat** Sandplains, floodplains and creek beds with cracking clay soils and a cover of woodlands, grasslands or sedges. **Status** Probably secure; sparse with seasonal population fluctuations. **Traces** Scats are similar to the Common Planigale. **Head-body** 44-75 mm. **Tail** 48-72 mm. **Weight** 4-10 g.

Common Planigale

Planigale maculata

A small, ferocious, carnivorous marsupial, the Common Planigale is cinnamon to grey-brown above, sometimes flecked with white; pale-brown to white below with a white chin. The head is triangular and flattened with small eyes and large ears with notched margins. The thin tail is shorter than the head and body. **Behaviour** Active mainly at night, Common Planigales sleep alone or with others in saucer-shaped nests lined with grass and shredded bark, in crevices, hollow logs, beneath bark or under rocks. They bask in the sun on cold days and become torpid for short periods when food is scarce. In the breeding season males fight frequently and scent-mark areas with their chest gland, probably establishing dominance hierarchies which give mating preferences to the largest. They are adept climbers and freeze if disturbed. **Development** Sexually mature at about 10 months, both sexes may breed for at least 2 years. The breeding season extends from October to January in eastern Australia with peaks in spring and summer, and lasts all year in the Northern Territory with several litters per year. Females have 8-13 teats in a rear-opening pouch, and give birth to 4-15 young 19-20 days after mating. Newborn attach firmly to the teats for about 21 days, vacating the pouch at 45 days, and remaining in the nest until weaned at about 70 days. **Diet** Insects and small vertebrates, some as large as themselves. **Habitat** Wet sites in rainforests, sclerophyll forests, shrublands, sedgelands and grasslands. **Status** Secure. **Traces** Scats are small twisted cylinders, about 1 mm across and 1-8 mm long, friable, packed with insect fragments. **Head-body** 65-100 mm. **Tail** 51-95 mm. **Weight** 6-22 g.

Planigale tenuirostris

Planigale maculata

Bilby

Macrotis lagotis

A delicately-built Rabbit-size marsupial of the desert regions, the Bilby has long, soft, silky fur, bluish-grey on the back, sandy-brown on the flanks and the end of the muzzle, whitish below and on the tip of the tail. The rest of the tail is black with a crest of hairs. The narrow head has large Rabbit-like ears, a long pointed snout and a long, slender tongue. The short forelimbs have no first digit, the others are long with strong curved claws. The hindfeet are long with a very large, strongly-clawed fourth toe; the second and third toes are fused with a double claw. **Behaviour** Strictly nocturnal, Bilbys are active mainly after midnight, sleeping in burrows up to 2 m deep and 3 m long spiralling steeply down, often with side tunnels and separate entrances; built in termite mounds, grass tussocks or below shrubs. Adult males have a number of exclusive burrows scent-marked by their anal glands, sometimes shared with one or more females and their young. A rigid dominance hierarchy is established among males without fighting, while females have a less rigid hierarchy and utter sharp growls in aggressive encounters. They have home ranges up to 14 ha, shifting according to the food supply. Their vision is poor, but they have acute hearing and sniff out insects and fungi, digging them up with their forefeet. Bilbys often stand upright sniffing the air, and run with a cantering gait with the tail held stiffly aloft, waving like a flag. **Development** Bilbys breed mainly from March to May, mating in the burrow and giving birth to 1-3 young after a pregnancy of 21 days. Females have 8 teats in a rear-opening pouch. Newborn attach firmly to the teats, vacate the pouch at 70-80 days, and are weaned some 14 days later. **Diet** Termites, ants, larvae, seeds, bulbs, fruit and fungi. They can survive without drinking. **Habitat** Arid and semi-arid shrublands, spinifex and tussock grasslands. **Status** Vulnerable; threatened by Fox and Cat predation and habitat destruction. **Traces** Conical diggings to 10 cm deep. Scats are often red-brown, smooth cylindrical pellets about 1 cm across and up to 25 mm long, deposited near diggings. **Head-body** 290-550 mm. **Tail** 200-290 mm. **Weight** 800-2500 g. Males are much larger than females.

Rufous Spiny Bandicoot

Echymipera rufescens

Found also in the rainforests of New Guinea, the Rufous Spiny Bandicoot is a Rabbit-size marsupial with coarse, stiff fur, rufous-brown flecked with black and grey above, becoming blacker on the shoulders and head; straw-coloured to white below. The tail is short, black and almost naked. The head is long and narrow with small eyes, small rounded ears and a long tapering snout with a naked tip. The short forelimbs have strong curved claws on elongated feet. The hindfeet are long with a very large, strongly-clawed fourth toe; the second and third toes are fused with a double claw for grooming. **Behaviour** Little studied, Rufous Spiny Bandicoots are nocturnal and strictly terrestrial, moving with a slow hop and a galloping run. They are thought to shelter in a burrow or in hollow logs and grass tussocks. They use their forefeet to dig conical holes searching for food, and investigate the hole with the snout. **Development** Little is known about their development. They probably breed in February. Females have a well-developed rear-opening pouch with 4 teats. **Diet** Insects, possibly small rodents, fruit and soft tubers. **Habitat** Tropical rainforests, vine forests, open forests, woodlands and adjoining heath. **Status** Probably secure. **Traces** Conical diggings at feeding sites. **Head-body** 300-400 mm. **Tail** 75-100 mm. **Weight** 450-2000 g. Males are larger than females.

Macrotis lagotis

Echymipera rufescens

Eastern Barred Bandicoot

Perameles gunnii

The Eastern Barred Bandicoot is a slender, graceful, Rabbit-size marsupial conspicu-
ously marked with 3-4 pale bars on each side of the rump. It has soft, dense fur,
mottled greyish-fawn above, paler on the flanks and pale grey to white below,
with prominent coarse guard hairs. The short pointed tail is white above with a
dark base. The elongated head has large pointed ears and small eyes. The short
forelimbs have strong, curved claws on long feet. The hindfeet are long with a very
large, strongly-clawed fourth toe, while the second and third toes are fused with a double claw
used for grooming. **Behaviour** Strictly nocturnal, they forage by night, digging for small invertebrates with the forefeet and probing with the snout. They sleep by day in simple domed nests of loose grass and
leaves over shallow depressions, concealed in dense undergrowth. Generally solitary, they use several nests and
Rabbit burrows for temporary shelter. Males have overlapping home ranges of around 13-26 ha. Females have
much smaller home ranges of around 2.5-4 ha. When alarmed they stand upright sniffing the air, and run with an
agile galloping or bounding gait, leaping up to 1 m. Vocalisations include snuffles, squeaks, hisses and grunts.
Development Sexually mature at 3-5 months, they may live to 3 years or more, breeding from winter to early
autumn with a peak from July to November. Females can raise 3-4 litters of 1-5 (usually 2-3) young per year. Born
only 12.5 days after mating, the young attach to some of the 8 teats in the mother's rear-opening pouch, which they
vacate after 48-55 days. They are then left in the nest while the mother forages until they are weaned at 70-80 days.
Juveniles disperse at 3-5 months. **Diet** Earthworms, insects, larvae, beetles, moths and other invertebrates, seeds,
roots, grass, fungi and some fruits. **Habitat** Savanna woodlands and tussock grasslands, preferring deep soils and
high rainfall. **Traces** Conical diggings about 10 cm wide and 15 cm deep, often with scats nearby. Scats are about
1 cm across and up to about 3 cm long, brown to black, friable with a smooth surface, containing insect remains and
soil particles. **Status** Vulnerable in Tas. and highly endangered on the mainland; threatened by Fox predation and
habitat destruction. **Head-body** 270-400 mm. **Tail** 70-110 mm. **Weight** 500-1450 g. Males are larger than females.

Southern Brown Bandicoot

Isoodon obesulus

The Southern Brown Bandicoot is a solidly-built, Rabbit-size marsupial with soft underfur and coarse, bristly guard hairs. The back is brownish-grey flecked with yellow-
brown and the belly creamy-white. The tail is short with a pointed tip, the head
long and tapering with a naked nose, small rounded ears and small eyes. The
short forelimbs have strong curved claws on elongated feet. The hindfeet are long
with a very large, strongly-clawed fourth toe; the second and third toes are fused
with a double claw used for grooming. **Behaviour** Active at night, they have a moderately fast,
agile galloping gait, and walk quadrupedally, foraging on the ground for insects and worms, digging
conical pits with the forefeet and probing with the snout. They sleep in an oval nest of leaf litter, grass, twigs and soil,
usually built in a shallow depression up to 75 cm long. Nests are sometimes found in decaying logs, Rabbit warrens,
or on a raised soil platform in wet sites. Generally solitary and aggressive, their survival depends on the establish-
ment of an adequate home range of up to 7 ha for males, and about 2 ha for females. Males range widely over areas
inhabited by several females, only interacting to mate. Squeaky grunts are made during aggressive encounters.
Development Sexually mature at 3-4 months, females begin breeding in the season following their birth, and may
live to 3 years or more. The breeding season extends from winter to the end of summer, coinciding with peaks in
food abundance, and may last all year in lowland heaths, with 2-3 litters being produced each year. Up to 6 young are
born 12.5 days after mating and attach to some of the 8 teats in the mother's rear-opening pouch. They are independent at 60-70 days, and the mother may give birth again as soon as the pouch is vacated. **Diet** Fungi, seeds and
invertebrates including ants, beetles, larvae and worms. **Habitat** Dry sclerophyll forests and woodlands, grasslands,
heaths, shrubland and regenerating areas with good ground cover, up to 1000 m. **Traces** Similar to the Eastern
Barred Bandicoot. **Status** Secure; vulnerable to land clearing and predation by Foxes. **Head-body** 275-360 mm.
Tail 90-140 mm. **Weight** 400-1600 g.

Perameles gunnii

Isoodon obesulus

Long-nosed Bandicoot

Perameles nasuta

A common visitor to suburban gardens, the Long-nosed Bandicoot is a compact,
Rabbit-size animal with greyish-brown fur flecked with dark-brown on its back, a
creamy-white belly and white feet. It has a short, pointed tail, a long head with a
slender muzzle and relatively long pointed ears. Its short forelimbs are designed
for digging, with long toes and strong, curved claws. The second and third toes of
the hindfeet are fused together with a double claw used for grooming, while the
fourth toe is longer and more powerful with a strong claw. **Behaviour** Nocturnal, they sleep in
well-concealed nests of dry grass and plant matter piled over shallow depressions, with a hollow centre but without a visible entrance. Soil is sometimes kicked over the top for camouflage and waterproofing. Rabbit
burrows are occasionally used. They forage on the ground for worms and insects, digging conical holes with the
forefeet and probing with the snout, often making shrill, grunt-like squeaks. They have a quadrupedal walk and can
move quite fast with a galloping gait. Adults are solitary and aggressively territorial; both sexes occupy separate
home ranges, often using different nests over several nights. Males establish dominance hierarchies and follow
females in the breeding season, waiting for a chance to mate. **Development** Sexually mature at 4-5 months, they
breed at any time with a lull from late autumn to mid-winter. Several litters of 1-5 (usually 2-3) young are reared per
year, born only 12.5 days after mating. Newborn are about 13 mm long and weigh about 0.25 g. They attach to the 8
teats in the mother's rear-opening pouch, opening their eyes at 45-50 days. They then leave the pouch and remain in
the nest until weaned at about 2 months. **Diet** Invertebrates such as worms, insects and larvae; eggs, fungi, seeds
and plant roots. **Habitat** Damp sites in rainforests, sclerophyll forests, woodlands, heaths and grasslands.
Traces Similar to the Eastern Barred Bandicoot. **Status** Secure. **Head-body** 310-430 mm. **Tail** 120-165 mm.
Weight 850-1100 g.

Northern Brown Bandicoot

Isoodon macrourus

Often found in suburban gardens, this Rabbit-size marsupial is dark-brown above
flecked with light-brown, and pale-grey to white below. The elongated head has relatively small pointed ears and small eyes. The tail is short and pointed. The forelimbs have strong curved claws on long feet. The hindfeet are long with a very
large, strongly-clawed fourth toe; the second and third toes are fused with a double claw used for grooming. **Behaviour** Nocturnal, Northern Brown Bandicoots
run with an agile galloping gait and walk quadrupedally, locating food by smell, digging conical holes with the forefeet and probing with the snout. Males are solitary and aggressive, marking areas
with a scent gland behind the ear and living in home ranges of 5-6 ha. Females occupy home ranges of 1-2 ha and
are followed persistently by males in the breeding season. They sleep in concealed nests of ground litter piled over
shallow depressions, with a hollow centre, loose entrance and exit, and soil kicked over the top for waterproofing.
They use several nests and sometimes shelter in hollow logs and grass tussocks. **Development** Sexually mature at
3-4 months, they live to 3 years, breeding throughout the year in Qld, from August to March in central NSW, and
August to April in the NT. Females rear several litters of 1-7 (usually 2-4) young per year, born only 12.5 days after
mating. They have 8 teats in a rear-opening pouch to which the young attach for about 50 days, thereafter remain-
ing in the nest until weaned at 2 months. **Diet** Insects, larvae, worms, berries, grass seeds and plant roots.
Habitat Woodlands, forests and grasslands with low ground cover. **Traces** Similar to the Eastern Barred Bandicoot.
Status Secure. **Head-body** 300-470 mm. **Tail** 80-215 mm. **Weight** 500-3100 g. Males are larger than females.

Perameles nasuta

Isoodon macrourus

Southern Hairy-nosed Wombat

Lasiorhinus latifrons

Distinguished from the Common Wombat by its silky fur, hairy nose and slightly smaller size, this large marsupial is grey to brownish-grey above and paler below. It has a broad, flattened head with narrow, pointed ears, small eyes, rodent-like incisor teeth and a split lip enabling it to pick emerging shoots. The tail is very short and hidden by fur. The limbs are short with short toes bearing stout, flattened claws for digging. The first toe of the hindfoot is very small, while the second and third toes are fused with a double claw used for grooming. **Behaviour** Nocturnal grazers, they move slowly and clumsily, but are very alert and can run with a bounding gait at up to 40 kph. They rest in deep humid burrows to conserve energy and water, and bask in the sun on winter days. Burrow entrances are clustered to form a large central warren with smaller warrens or single burrows surrounding it. Each warren system is occupied by 5-10 Wombats.and covers an area 200-300 m across, connected by a network of tracks marked at intervals with urine, scats and scratching. Males generally stay in the central warren and females move between warrens. Males establish dominance hierarchies and are aggressive in the breeding season. Mating takes place in the burrow. **Development** Sexually mature at 3 years, they live for more than 20 years in captivity. The breeding season extends from late September to December, but they do not breed in droughts, and need 2-3 years of rainfall to successfully raise the young. Usually a single young is born and attaches to one of 2 teats in the mother's rear-opening pouch, emerging 6-9 months later, and following the mother until weaned at one year. **Diet** Grasses and herbs. They can survive for long periods without drinking. **Habitat** Arid and semi-arid grasslands and open woodlands with 200-500 mm of rain. **Traces** Scats are cube-shaped pellets about 2 cm across, dark-brown outside, comprising fine green plant fragments, deposited in groups of 4-8 near burrows, pathways and feeding sites. **Status** Endangered; threatened by land clearing, overgrazing and habitat destruction. **Head-body** 770-940 mm. **Tail** 25-60 mm. **Weight** 19-32 kg.

Common Wombat

Vombatus ursinus

A large, squat burrowing marsupial, with long, coarse, stiff fur, patchy brownish-grey or dull sandy-brown above and paler below. It has a large, broad head with a flattened, naked nose, small eyes and small, hairy ears; and a very short tail hidden by fur. Its short forelimbs are adapted for digging with short toes bearing stout flattened claws. The first toe of the hindfoot is just a stub, while the second and third toes are fused with a double claw used for grooming. **Behaviour** Solitary and aggressive, they are mainly nocturnal, although they graze during the day in winter, in overlapping home ranges of 4-24 ha, travelling up to 3 km overnight. They have poor eyesight but acute hearing and smell, and scent-mark and defend separate feeding sites They shelter in burrows up to 30 m long, often with several entrances and nesting chambers with connecting tunnels, usually dug in slopes above creeks and gullies. Shorter burrows 2-5 m long are used for temporary refuge. Burrows are dug in a common area and some are used by different individuals. The entrances are usually 40-50 cm across with mounds of soil outside and well-worn pathways between them. Individuals use more than 10 burrows, visiting 1-4 burrows each night and alternating between 3 major sleeping burrows. If the ground is hard they shelter in caves and hollow logs. Although seemingly slow and clumsy, they can bound at 40 kph over short distances. A male trots behind a female during courtship in circles and figure of eight patterns until she allows him to copulate. **Development** Sexually mature at 2 years, they breed year-round on the mainland, with a peak from September to November; and in winter in Tasmania. Usually a single young weighing about 0.5 g is born, and attaches to one of the 2 teats in the mother's rear-opening pouch. It leaves the pouch at 6-10 months and stays in the burrow, suckling until about 15 months old, and then remains at heel until about 20 months. Females mate again when weaning is complete, usually giving birth once every 2 years. Wombats may live for 15 years or more. **Diet** Tussock grasses, some introduced grasses, rushes and sedges; supplemented with roots, tubers, mosses and fungi. **Habitat** Wet and dry open forests woodlands, scrubs and wet heaths to 1800 m. **Traces** Scats are cube-shaped pellets about 2 cm across, dark-brown outside, comprising fine green plant fragments, usually deposited in groups of 4-8 in conspicuous places. **Status** Secure; protected in western Vic., but declining in numbers due to habitat destruction and competition from stock. **Head-body** 850-1200 mm. **Tail** 20-30 mm. **Weight** 22-39 kg.

Lasiorhinus latifrons

Vombatus ursinus

Rock Ringtail Possum

Petropseudes dahli

A Rabbit-sized marsupial with long woolly fur, grey to brownish-grey above with a dark stripe from forehead to rump, white below with white patches around the eye and under the ear. The short, prehensile tail is thick at the base and tapers to a thin, nearly naked terminal half. The head is pointed with a naked nose and small rounded ears. The legs are short with short claws on hands and feet. The first 2 fingers of the forefeet oppose the other 3. The hindfeet have an opposing first toe; the second and third are fused with a double claw for grooming. **Behaviour** Active at night, Rock Ringtail Possums feed in trees and shrubs, usually among rocks, and sleep by day on well-protected rock ledges, in clefts and fissures. They are usually seen on or near rocks in pairs or family groups, touching each other frequently. Adults mark rocks and tree branches with secretions from their chest and anal glands, presumably to define a territory. They are shy and run for cover when caught in a spotlight, sometimes hiding their head in a rock cleft, leaving the body exposed. The least arboreal of the ringtail possums, they are nevertheless good climbers and leapers; on the ground they walk and run on all-fours, and sit on their tail when resting. Vocalisations include quiet screeches and grunts. **Development** Rock Ringtail Possums are thought to breed year-round, and females with large pouch young have been seen from March to September. They give birth to a single young that attaches to one of 2 teats in the mother's forward-opening pouch. Young ride on the mother's back after leaving the pouch, and spend time at heel before becoming independent. **Diet** Leaves, flowers and fruits of trees and shrubs. **Habitat** Rocky escarpments and outcrops with deep fissures in open forest and vine forest thickets. **Traces** Bright red eyeshine, does not freeze in a spotlight. Scats are reddish-brown to black, banana-shaped, 15-25 mm long and about 5 mm across, usually deposited in groups of 3-6. **Status** Probably secure. **Head-body** 330-385 mm. **Tail** 200-266 mm. **Weight** 1.2-2 kg.

Koala

Phascolarctos cinereus

The koala is a short, stocky, largely arboreal marsupial with fine woolly fur, grey with brown and white patches and a white to yellowish chest and belly. It has a broad, flat head with large hairy ears, a naked flattened nose and small eyes. Although the koala's tail is no more than a stump, it is well adapted to an arboreal life with long limbs and strongly-clawed feet, enabling it to climb trees by digging its claws into the trunk. Powerful, opposing, thumb-like first digits on the hindfeet can grip against the other toes. The forefeet have an unusual split-hand arrangement; the first 2 digits oppose the other 3, giving it a vice-like grip on branches. For grooming it has a double claw on the fused second and third toes of the hindfeet. In subtropical and tropical districts they are smaller with shorter fur. **Behaviour** Solitary and nocturnal, koalas spend much of their time resting or feeding in the upper branches of gum trees. They climb slowly, grasping the trunk with the forefeet and pulling the hindlimbs up, and can jump up to 2 m between branches. On the ground they walk on all-fours, run with a bounding gait, and can swim if necessary. Koalas spend most of their lives within a home range, averaging about 1.7 ha for males and about 1.2 ha for females. Home ranges often overlap and males roam around, establishing dominance hierarchies, communicating their status by bellowing and marking trees with secretions from their chest gland. Juveniles disperse at about 2 years of age. Young females sometimes settle near their mother, but young males usually become nomadic for 2-3 years. **Development** Koalas are sexually mature at the end of their second year, but males are unable to compete for females until they are 4-5 years old. They mate in trees and usually give birth to a single young, mostly in early summer, 34-36 days after mating. Newborn attach to one of 2 teats in the mother's rear-opening pouch, which they vacate at 6-7 months, riding on the mother's back until weaned at 11-12 months. Koalas have a lifespan of 10-15 years (when their teeth wear out). **Diet** Leaves from a range of eucalypt trees, sometimes supplemented by Radiata Pine, Camphor Laurel and Coast Tea Tree. They can survive without drinking in winter. **Habitat** Eucalypt forests and woodlands. **Traces** Claw scratches and pock marks on tree trunks, scats around the base. Scats are oval or cylindrical, mostly brown or red-brown, about 1 cm across and 2-3 cm long with a ridged surface, packed with coarse leaf fragments. **Status** Vulnerable; threatened by habitat fragmentation, land clearing, logging, road kills and attacks by domestic Dogs. **Head-body** 648-820 mm. **Weight** 4-13.5 kg. Males are larger than females.

Petropseudes dahli

Phascolarctos cinereus

POSSUMS

Herbert River Ringtail Possum   *Pseudochirulus herbertensis*

An arboreal marsupial of the dense tropical rainforests, the Herbert River Ringtail
Possum has dark-brown to black fur with white or cream markings on the chest,
belly and upper forearm. Some adults have no white fur, while juveniles are
pale-fawn and have a stripe along their upper head and back. It has a long
pointed face, small rounded ears, bulging eyes and a narrow, tapering, prehensile tail carried in a coil. To help it grip branches the first 2 fingers of the forefeet
oppose the other 3, the hindfeet have an opposing first toe, while the second and third toes are
fused with a double claw used for grooming. **Behaviour** Active at night, they are agile, cautious
climbers, making small, careful leaps through the canopy, and rarely descending to the ground where they walk on
all-fours. They sleep by day in dens in tree hollows, fern clumps or dense vegetation, sometimes building rough
spherical nests using shredded bark or other vegetation carried in the curled tail. They are generally solitary and
occupy overlapping home ranges of 0.5-1 ha. During the breeding season a female on heat is accompanied by a con-
sort male who stays close to her throughout the night, shadowing her for up to 48 days until she allows him to mate.
Vocalisations consist of quiet clicks, grunts and screeches. **Development** Herbert River Ringtail Possums mate
from March to December with a peak in May-July, usually producing one litter of twins each year. Newborn attach
to the 2 developed teats in the mother's forward-opening pouch, which they vacate at 105-120 days. Young ride on
the mother's back for 2 weeks, and are then left in the nest until weaned at 150-160 days. **Diet** Leaves, supplemented with flowers and fruits. **Habitat** Rainforest above 300 m and occasionally tall open eucalypt forest.
Traces Bright pinkish-orange eyeshine at night. Scats are dark, about 5 mm across and 15 mm long, containing fine
plant fragments. **Status** Vulnerable; sparsely distributed, threatened by land clearing. **Head-body** 300-400 mm.
Tail 290-470 mm. **Weight** 800-1530 g.

Common Ringtail Possum   *Pseudocheirus peregrinus*

Often seen in suburban gardens, this Rabbit-size arboreal marsupial has a grey back,
sometimes rufous-tinged, white to bright-rufous underparts, pale patches below the
ears and eyes, and rufous-tinged legs. It has a long, white-tipped prehensile tail
carried in a loose coil when not in use, bare for some distance below to help it
grip branches. Other arboreal adaptations include strongly clawed feet with the
first 2 fingers of the forefoot and the first toe of the hindfoot opposing the others.
The second and third toes of the hindfeet are fused with a long, split claw used for grooming.
Behaviour Active at night, they spend most of their time foraging and grooming in trees and leaping
between branches. On the ground they move on all-fours and can swim well. They rest in spherical nests around
300-350 mm diameter with a circular entrance, built in the fork of a tree or shrub using woven twigs, leaves, fern
fronds and grass, lined with shredded bark, moss or grass. Tree hollows are used, but only when available, allowing
them to exploit a variety of vegetation types. They live in family groups comprising an adult male with one or occasionally 2 adult females and offspring from the previous breeding season. Families build and use a number of nests
and occupy a common home range. Juveniles are forced to disperse and establish their own home ranges. The home
ranges of females overlap, while males tend to have exclusive home ranges. They emit soft, high-pitched twittering
calls and when handled they secrete a strong-smelling liquid from their anal glands. **Development** Sexually mature
at about 13 months, they have a lifespan of 3-6 years. Litters vary from 1-4, but usually 2 young are born from late
April to November, and 2 litters a year may be raised. Newborn attach to one of the 4 teats in the mother's forward-
opening pouch for 42-49 days. They leave the pouch at about 4 months and are left in the nest for the next 2 weeks or
carried on their mother's back while she forages. They then nest with their father who cares for them until they are
weaned at 5-8 months. **Diet** Eucalypt and other leaves, flowers and fruits. Soft faecal pellets of partially digested
food are produced during the day and eaten immediately. **Habitat** Forests, woodlands, rainforests, tea tree thickets
and dense shrublands, to above 1200 m. **Traces** Claw marks on tree trunks; small groups of scats, chewed leaves and
blossoms at base. Scats are red-brown to green, cylindrical with rounded ends, 5-8 mm across and about 15 mm long.
Status Secure. **Head-body** 300-350 mm. **Tail** 300-350 mm. **Weight** 660-1100 g.

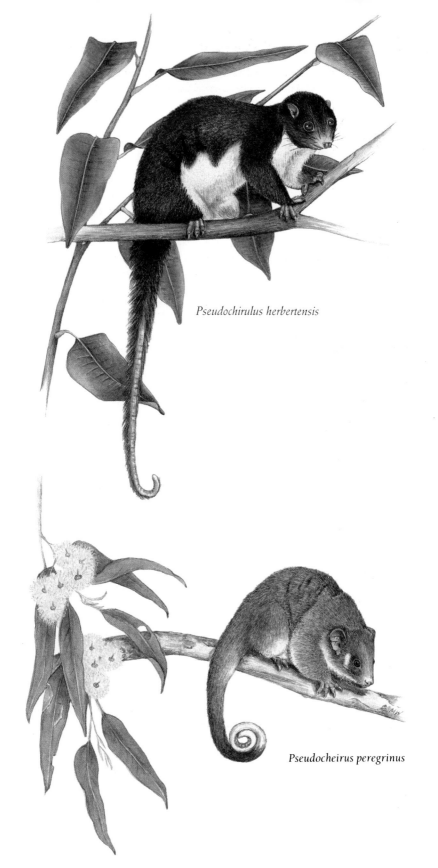

Pseudochirulus herbertensis

Pseudocheirus peregrinus

Lemuroid Ringtail Possum

Hemibelideus lemuroides

A predominantly arboreal marsupial usually found high in the forest canopy, the Lemuroid Ringtail Possum has soft fur, uniformly dark charcoal-grey above, sometimes brownish on the shoulders and lighter below with a yellowish tinge. Some animals are creamy-white with a tinge of orange on the shoulders. The face is short with a roman nose and small ears. The long prehensile tail is bushy, slightly tapered with a short, naked, finger-like tip, coiled when not used. To help them grip branches the first 2 fingers of the hands oppose the other 3 and the hindfeet have an opposing first toe. The second and third toes are fused together with a double claw used for grooming. **Behaviour** Strictly nocturnal, Lemuroid Ringtail Possums sleep in dens in tree hollows, often sharing with other members of the same family. They very gregarious and are often seen at night in pairs or family groups, sometimes feeding in a tree with other groups or individuals. They are noisy animals, frequently leaping 2-3 m through the canopy with their legs outstretched like a glider and crashing into the foliage. They occasionally emit loud screams and wails and produce a musky-smelling, sticky, creamy-coloured secretion from their anal glands when handled. On the ground they move on all-fours. **Development** Lemuroid Ringtail Possums breed from June to November, producing a single young that attaches to one of 2 teats in the mother's well-developed, forward-opening pouch. The young ride on their mother's back after emerging from the pouch, and if separated emit a high-pitched squeaking distress signal. **Diet** Mainly leaves, supplemented by flowers and fruits. **Habitat** Tropical rainforests above 450 m. **Traces** Brilliant white-yellow eyeshine at night. Scats are dark oval to cylindrical pellets about 5 mm across and 10 mm long, packed with fine plant material. **Status** Vulnerable; threatened by clearing of rainforests. **Head-body** 310-360 mm. **Tail** 300-375 mm. **Weight** 750-1300 g.

Green Ringtail Possum

Pseudochirops archeri

A Rabbit-sized arboreal marsupial of dense upland rainforests, the Green Ringtail Possum has thick soft fur, greyish-green to lime-green above with 2 silvery-yellow stripes from the shoulders to the rump on each side of the spine. It is white below with white patches around the eyes and ears. The pointed head has a pink nose, bulging eyes and small rounded ears. Arboreal adaptations include a relatively short prehensile tail with a thick base tapering to a narrow tip that is curled up when not used, and opposing fingers and toes for gripping. The first 2 digits of the forefeet oppose the other 3, while the hindfeet have an opposing first toe and fused second and third toes with a double claw for grooming. **Behaviour** Green Ringtail Possums are active mainly at night, although if disturbed they may feed and move during the day. Most of their active time is spent high up in the canopy where they move with surprising speed and agility, running along branches and up vines, but avoiding leaping. They only descend to the ground to move between trees, moving on all-fours. They sleep upright on a branch among the foliage, curled into a tight ball with the tail coiled under the chin, gripping the branch with their hindfeet. The Green Ringtail Possum is perhaps the most solitary of the ringtails, although mothers with young at heel and pairs of mating adults are occasionally seen. Adults are silent, but pouch young utter a quiet "tssk tssk tssk" when handled. **Development** Sexually mature at about 12 months, they probably breed all year with a peak from July to November, giving birth to a single young that attaches to one of 2 teats in the mother's forward-opening pouch. Young ride on the mother's back after vacating the pouch. **Diet** Leaves, mainly of fig trees. Soft faecal pellets of partially digested food are produced during the day and consumed immediately. **Habitat** Dense tropical rainforest above 300 m. **Status** Vulnerable; threatened by clearing of rainforest. **Head-body** 285-380 mm. **Tail** 310-372 mm. **Weight** 670-1350 g.

Hemibelideus lemuroides

Pseudochirops archeri

Southern Common Cuscus
Phalanger intercastellanus

Previously known as the Grey Cuscus, this species is a relatively lightly-built arboreal marsupial of the northern tropical rainforests. It has soft woolly fur, grey-brown above and off-white below, with a brown stripe from the ears to the rump. Males have a distinct yellowish chest gland and a yellow tinge on the side of the neck. The triangular head has bulging, forward-facing eyes and small, round, project- ing ears. Arboreal adaptation include a long prehensile tail, naked for two-thirds of its length with a rough, gripping undersurface, and grasping forefeet with the first 2 toes oppos- ing the other 3. They have strong curved claws and long canine teeth. **Behaviour** Cryptic and soli- tary, Southern Common Cuscuses sleep in dens in tree hollows during the day and climb slowly and deliberately through the canopy at night, leaping across gaps, gripping branches with the forefeet and using the tail as a fifth limb. On the ground they move with a slow bounding gait. Males are probably territorial, using their chest gland to scent-mark areas. Vocalisations include harsh aggressive guttural screeches, grunts and clicks. **Development** The Southern Common Cuscus probably breeds throughout the year. Females usually give birth to twins that attach to 2 of the 4 teats in the mother's forward-opening, well-developed pouch. Infants are carried on the mother's back after vacating the pouch. Males grow throughout their life. **Diet** Leaves, fruits, flowers, buds and seeds. **Habitat** Rain- forests at all elevations. **Traces** Bright red eyeshine at night. **Status** Vulnerable; threatened by clearing of rain- forests. **Head-body** 350-400 mm. **Tail** 280-350 mm. **Weight** 1.5-2.2 kg.

Spotted Cuscus
Spilocuscus maculatus

An arboreal marsupial of the northern tropical rainforests, the Spotted Cuscus is heav- ily-built with a very short snout and a flat round face with large, forward-pointing, red-rimmed eyes. The dense woolly fur is grey above and creamy-white below and hides the small ears. Males have irregular creamy-white spots on the back, while females are more uniformly grey, usually with a white rump. The long, strongly prehensile tail is naked for the terminal two-thirds with a rough undersurface for extra grip, and is coiled up tightly when not in use. The feet have strong curved claws and the first 2 toes of the forefeet oppose the other 3 enabling it to grasp branches. They have long canine teeth.
Behaviour Active mainly at night and on cool, overcast days, the Spotted Cuscus is usually seen alone, resting on exposed branches in dense clumps of foliage, or sleeping on a small temporary platform of leaves and twigs pulled underneath itself, rarely returning to the same tree the following day. Males are territorial and aggressively defend an area defined by scent-marking. They climb slowly and deliberate through the canopy, sometimes leaping between trees, holding branches in a vice-like grip with the feet and using the tail as a fifth limb. On the ground they move with a bounding gait and may travel a few hundred metres. Vocalisations include hisses, screeches, grunts and clicks. If stressed they secrete a reddish-brown substance on the bare facial skin, particularly around the eyes.
Development Spotted Cuscuses probably breed throughout the year, usually giving birth to 1-2 young that attach to some of the 4 teats in the mother's forward-opening, well-developed pouch. Infants are carried on the mother's back after vacating the pouch. **Diet** Leaves, fruits, insects and probably small birds and mammals. **Habitat** Mainly rain- forests from sea-level to 820 m, some open forests and mangroves. **Traces** Scats are brown cylindrical pellets up to 1 cm across and 2-3 cm long, comprising coarse plant material. **Status** Vulnerable; threatened by rainforest clear- ing. **Head-body** 350-580 mm. **Tail** 315-435 mm. **Weight** 1.5-4.9 kg.

Phalanger intercastellanus

Spilocuscus maculatus

Scaly-tailed Possum

Wyulda squamicaudata

A Rabbit-size arboreal marsupial and the only member of the genus, the Scaly-tailed
Possum lives in rugged, rocky terrain and has affinities with the Brushtail Possums
and the Cuscus. It has pale-grey fur on the back with a slightly darker stripe
running from the crown to the rump. It is creamy-white below and sometimes
rufous around the base of the prehensile tail, which is naked for most of its
length with prominent scales. The head is quite long with a flattened pink nose,
small ears and large bulging eyes. The hindfeet have an opposing first toe for grasping
branches, while the second and third toes are fused with a double claw used for grooming.
Behaviour Scaly-tailed Possums sleep by day in rock crevices or deep within rock piles. They emerge at night to
feed on the ground and in trees where they are agile climbers, gripping branches with their hindfeet and using the
prehensile tail as a fifth limb. They are solitary, with a home range some 250 m wide. **Development** Females are
sexually mature at about 2 years, males at 18 months. Females usually give birth in the dry season from March to
August, although a mother with a small pouch young has been trapped in January. The single young remains in the
mother's forward-opening pouch for 147-200 days, and is weaned at about 35 weeks. **Diet** Leaves, blossoms, fruits,
seeds and insects. **Habitat** Open and closed forests and vine thickets in rugged, rocky terrain with more than
900 mm of rain annually. **Status** Vulnerable; restricted to a limited area. **Head-body** 290-400 mm. **Tail** 255-350 mm.
Weight 1.2-2 kg.

Mountain Brushtail Possum

Trichosurus caninus

A relatively large and robust arboreal marsupial, the Mountain Brushtail Possum is
flecked steel-grey above and whitish below. It has short, rounded ears and a pink
nose. Arboreal adaptations include a black, bushy, curved and tapering prehensile tail with a bare section beneath the tip, and clawless opposing first toes on
the hindfeet for gripping. The forefeet have 5 strongly-clawed, non-opposing fingers, while the second and third toes of the hindfeet are fused with a long, split
claw used for grooming. Animals in north eastern districts are dark-grey to deep amber-
brown above. **Behaviour** Active mainly at night, Mountain Brushtail Possums move rapidly through
the trees, often crashing through the canopy and frequently descending to the ground to feed. They walk on all-
fours with a rolling gait with the hindfeet turned out, and can swim if necessary. They sleep in dens in tree hollows,
hollow logs, stumps or occasionally in large epiphytic ferns. Most adults use more than one den and both sexes
have overlapping home ranges of about 7 ha for males and 5 ha for females. Home ranges are marked with secretions of scent glands located under the chin, on the chest, and below the base of the tail. Adults form monogamous
pairs and share a home range for most of the year. Juveniles disperse when they are 18-36 months old. They are
usually relatively quiet and docile, emitting guttural snorts when disturbed. **Development** Males are sexually
mature at 30-36 months, females at 2 years. The breeding season extends from February to May. A single young is
born 15-17 days after conception. It attaches to one of 2 teats in the mother's forward-facing pouch, which it vacates
5-6 months later, riding on the mother's back until weaned at 8-9 months. Males have a lifespan of up to 12 years,
and females to 17 years. **Diet** Leaves, fungi, lichen, bark and pine cones. **Habitat** Tall, wet sclerophyll forests and
rainforests with a good understorey. **Traces** Claw marks on trees. Scats are about 10 mm across and 15-25 mm
long, brown, comprising coarse plant fragments, often found on fallen logs and around trees. **Status** Secure.
Head-body 400-570 mm. **Tail** 340-420 mm. **Weight** 2.2-4.5 kg.

Wyulda squamicaudata

Trichosurus caninus

Common Brushtail Possum

Trichosurus vulpecula

A Rabbit-size arboreal marsupial, usually silver-grey above and off-white to cream below, with large pointed ears, dark patches on the muzzle and white patches below the ears. The tail is black, bushy, relatively short and moderately prehensile with a naked area beneath the tip. A clawless opposing first toe on the hindfoot helps it grip branches, while the second and third toes are fused with a long, split claw for grooming. A north Queensland subspecies has short, coppery-coloured fur, and Tasmanian animals are larger with denser fur. **Behaviour** Common Brushtail Possums are nocturnal and agile climbers using their tail, sharp claws, and opposing toes to grasp branches. Tree hollows, logs, dense undergrowth, Rabbit holes and roof spaces are used as dens. Adults are solitary for most of the year, and mark their den sites and home ranges with secretions from scent glands on the chin, chest and anal region. Individuals use several dens, moving between them during the year, and some may be used independently by other possums. Dens are shared during the breeding season or by a mother and her young. Adults often travel long distances on the ground and establish home ranges up to 7 h for males and 5 ha for females. Dominant males have larger home ranges often overlapping those of several females. Young females establish a home range adjacent to their mother's, while young males disperse. Their large vocal repertoire includes guttural coughs, sharp hisses, loud chattering and screeching. **Development** Females may give birth in their first year and males are fertile by the end of their second year. Breeding occurs year round in the north, with peaks in autumn and spring in other areas. In good conditions females may give birth twice in a year, producing a single young 16-18 days after mating. It attaches to one of 2 teats in the mother's forward-opening pouch, remaining attached for about 94 days and leaving the pouch at 4-5 months. It is then left in the den or rides on its mother's back until 7-9 months old. They may live for up to 13 years. **Diet** Leaves, fruits, blossoms, grass, insects. **Habitat** Dry and moderately wet sclerophyll forests, woodlands and urban areas. **Traces** Claw marks on trees. Scats are red-brown to black, 3-10 mm wide and 20-30 mm long, deposited in groups or strings, sometimes containing insect remains. **Status** Secure; protected on the mainland; rare and endangered in central Australia. **Head-body** 350-550 mm. **Tail** 250-400 mm. **Weight** 1.2-4.5 kg. Males are usually larger.

Leadbeater's Possum

Gymnobelideus leadbeateri

Once presumed extinct, this arboreal marsupial was rediscovered in 1961. It has soft fur, grey to greyish-brown above and paler below, with a dark-brown stripe along the back. The large thin ears have a small white patch at the base. Arboreal adaptations include a thick prehensile tail with a broad, bushy tip, a clawless opposable first toe on the hindfoot, large gripping footpads and retractable claws. The second and third toes are partly joined with a double claw for grooming. **Behaviour** Shy and secretive, they emerge from at dusk and move rapidly through the canopy, leaping between trees and climbing smooth trunks with ease. Up to three quarters of their time is spent in a communal nest more than 250 mm across, made of shredded bark and built in the hollow centre of a large tree with a narrow access hole. Colony members make nests in 2-3 trees about 50 m apart and often move between them, defending a surrounding territory of 1-2 ha against adjacent colonies. Up to 8 animals live in a colony, with a monogamous breeding pair, their offspring, and sometimes an extra male. They groom each other frequently, recognise each other by smell and make hissing and chattering noises. Females are more aggressive than males and evict their daughters at 10 months, forcing them to establish a new colony or join one which has lost its resident breeding female. Males disperse at about 15 months and join a neighbouring colony or a bachelor group until mating opportunities arise. **Development** Females are sexually mature at 10 months, males at 15 months. Most births occur in May-June or October-November. Females have 4 teats in a rear-opening pouch and give birth to 1-2 young. They attach to the teats and remain in the pouch for 80-93 days, emerging from the nest at about 110 days to forage alone. **Diet** Beetles, spiders, and other invertebrates extracted from shedding bark; honeydew, and plant secretions. **Habitat** Tall, open, montane forests, mainly Mountain Ash, with a dense understorey and large old or dead trees. **Traces** Scats are about 3 mm across and 20 mm long, friable, containing fine powdery particles, with a strong, sweet odour when fresh. **Status** Endangered; threatened by logging of old trees. **Head-body** 150-170 mm. **Tail** 145-180 mm. **Weight** 100-166 g.

Trichosurus vulpecula

Gymnobelideus leadbeateri

Greater Glider

Petauroides volans

The largest of the gliding possums, the Greater Glider is whitish below and dark-grey, dusky-brown, cream or greyish-white above. It has large ears with a furry fringe, a short snout and a long, bushy and weakly-prehensile, pendulous tail. A square membrane joins the flanks, elbows and ankles and acts as a wing when the limbs are extended. The feet are designed to grip onto branches: the first 2 toes of the forefeet oppose the other 3 and the hindfeet have an opposing first toe. A long, split claw on the fused second and third toes of the hindfeet is used for grooming. **Behaviour** Active at night, Greater Gliders emerge at dusk from dens high up in tree hollows, and follow established routes to feeding sites. They are generally solitary, although during the mating season pairs often share dens until the young leave the pouch. Males and females occupy individual home ranges of 1-6 ha, defined by scent-marking trees with anal gland secretions and urine. Male home ranges never overlap, but female home ranges often overlap those of males or other females, and in good habitats males may have exclusive access to several females. They are agile climbers and can glide more than 100 m, extending the limbs, bringing the paws under the chin and steering with the tail and gliding membrane. On the ground they have a clumsy loping gait. Females returning to the den after foraging communicate with their nestlings with high-pitched twittering sounds. **Development** Males are sexually mature at 12 months, females at 18 months. Mating takes place from March to June. A single young is born and attaches to one of 2 teats in the mother's forward-opening pouch. The infant leaves the pouch at 3-4 months and for the next 3 months is left in the den or rides on the mother's back while she climbs, but not while gliding. Young are independent at 8-10 months. **Diet** Eucalypt leaves and buds, and occasionally mistletoe. They can survive without drinking. **Habitat** Wet and dry sclerophyll forests and tall woodlands with old hollow trees, from sea-level to above 1200 m. **Traces** Strongly reflective eyeshine at night. Scratches made on tree trunks when landing. Scats are found under den trees. They are pellets, 5-10 mm across, red-brown to brown, comprising fine leaf particles. **Status** Probably secure; vulnerable to logging and lack of nesting sites in old, hollow trees.
Head-body 350-450 mm. **Tail** 450-600 mm. **Weight** 900-1800 g.

Squirrel Glider

Petaurus norfolcensis

Larger, but otherwise similar to the Sugar Glider, this species is light-grey above with a dark stripe along the forehead and back. It is white to creamy-white below with white markings on the cheeks and behind the ears. The prehensile tail is broad, long, bushy and soft with a dark tip. It has large protruding eyes, large ears, a pointed snout and a rectangular gliding membrane between the hands and feet. The feet are grasping: the first 2 toes of the forefeet oppose the other 3 and the hindfeet have an opposing first toe. A double claw on the fused second and third toes of the hindfeet is used for grooming. **Behaviour** Active mainly at night, Squirrel Gliders are agile climbers and can glide more than 50 m between trees. They forage mainly in the upper canopy, gleaning insects from the foliage and licking sap from gashes made with their sharp incisor teeth in the bark of eucalypt and wattle trees. They build bowl-shaped, leaf-lined nests in tree hollows, utilising a number of hollows and travelling up to 1 km from preferred hollows to foraging sites. They nest alone, in pairs or in family groups comprising one mature male, one or more adult females, and their offspring of the season. Males have well-developed scent glands and family groups occupy home ranges of 20-30 ha. Vocalisations include gurgling chatter and soft grunts. **Development** Sexually mature at about 12 months, Squirrel Gliders mate from May to December, often giving birth to twins. Newborn attach to 2 of the 4 teats in the mother's forward-opening pouch. They vacate the pouch at about 70 days and are left in the nest for another 30 days before accompanying the mother on foraging trips until weaned at about 120 days. **Diet** Caterpillars, weevils, beetles, moths, supplemented with sap, nectar, pollen, small birds, eggs and sometimes mice. **Habitat** Sclerophyll forests and woodlands. **Traces** horizontal and vertical gashes on tree trunks. Scats are found at the base of trees. They are roughly formed cylinders less than 5 mm across and 10-15 mm long, with a dark, shiny surface, usually friable, containing insect fragments and powdery particles. **Status** Vulnerable; sparse with a patchy distribution; threatened by land clearing and predation by Cats and Foxes. **Head-body** 170-240 mm. **Tail** 220-300 mm. **Weight** 170-300 g.

Petauroides volans

Petaurus norfolcensis

Sugar Glider

Petaurus breviceps

This small gliding possum is light grey above with a distinct dark stripe along its fore-head and back, and dark patches behind its large pointed ears. It is creamy-white to pale-grey below with short body fur and a bushy prehensile tail, sometimes white-tipped. A square gliding membrane joins the fifth finger and the first toe. The feet are able to grasp branches; the first 2 digits of the forefeet oppose the other 3, and the hindfeet have an opposing first toe. The second and third toes of the hindfeet are fused and have a split claw used for grooming. **Behaviour** Active mainly at night, Sugar Gliders are shy, fast, agile climbers and can glide more than 50 m. They build communal spherical or bowl-shaped nests of eucalypt leaves in tree hollows, shared by up to 7 adults and their young of the season. A typical social group comprises 3-4 adult females and 2-3 adult males. One male is dominant and scent-marks other group members and the group's territorial boundaries with secretions from glands on his forehead, chest and at the base of his tail. Territories of up to 7 ha and favourite food trees are defended. Young males are forced to disperse, but young females sometimes remain to replace females lost to the group. In very cold, wet weather they huddle together in the nest and become torpid for short periods. Vocalisations include a loud bark or 'yip' when alarmed and a rolling guttural anger call. **Development** Females become sexually mature at 8-15 months, males at 12 months. They have a life expectancy of 4-5 years in the wild and breed from June to November, rearing up to 2 litters per season. Twins are usually born 16 days after mating and attach to 2 of 4 teats in the forward-opening pouch for 40 days, emerging at 60-70 days. Young remain in the nest for another 50 days, and forage with their mother until 7-10 months old. **Diet** Acacia gum and eucalypt sap licked from gashes in tree trunks made with their lower incisor teeth, nectar, pollen, manna, honeydew, beetles, moths, spiders and other invertebrates, and occasionally small birds and mam-mals. **Habitat** Wet and dry eucalypt forests and woodlands, usually with wattles, from sea level to over 1200 m. **Traces** Similar to the Squirrel Glider. **Status** Secure. **Head-body** 150-210 mm. **Tail** 165-210 mm. **Weight** 95-170 g.

Yellow-bellied Glider

Petaurus australis

This Rabbit-size gliding possum is dark to pale grey-brown above, off-white to yellow-orange below, with dark stripes along the mid-back and thigh, and dark limbs. The ears are large, pointed and almost naked and a square gliding membrane joins the wrists and ankles. Arboreal adaptations include a long, broad and bushy prehen-sile tail and grasping feet: the first 2 digits of the forefeet oppose the other 3, and the hindfeet have an opposing first toe. The second and third toes of the hindfeet are fused with a split claw used for grooming. **Behaviour** Active mainly at night, Yellow-bellied Gliders are fast and very agile, running beneath branches and gliding up to 120 m between trees. They travel more than 2 km for food, occasionally feeding in small groups in the same tree. Their social behaviour is among the most complex of any marsupial studied, and includes a wide range of vocalisations from loud gurgling shrieks to growls, whoos and rattling chatter. They pair for life and live and move in family groups, sometimes with more than one breeding female. Groups live in large hollows, building substantial spherical nests of eucalypt leaves carried in the coiled tail. Each group uses several hollows (although individuals do not always share the same den) within an exclu-sive home range of 30-60 ha. Adult males scent-mark family members with secretions from glands on the forehead, chest and base of the tail. **Development** Mating often takes place while clinging to the underside of a branch. Births occur at any time of year with peaks from August to September in the south and May to September in the north. Usually a single young is born and attaches to one of 2 teats in the forward-opening pouch, where it stays for 90-100 days, remaining in the nest for another 40-50 days, becoming independent at 6-8 months. Both parents help to raise the young, and juveniles remain with their parents until sexually mature at 18-24 months, when they disperse. They have a lifespan of 14 years or more. **Diet** Nectar, pollen, insects, manna, honeydew and eucalypt sap obtained by bit-ing into the bark. **Habitat** Wet and dry eucalypt forests and woodlands, often in mountainous areas. **Traces** Deep, V-shaped slashes in eucalypt bark; oval pellets of chewed bark on the ground. Scats are dark brown, shiny, about 5 mm across and 15 mm long, containing fine powdery material and sometimes insect remains. **Status** Vulnerable; threat-ened by logging practices. **Head-body** 270-320 mm. **Tail** 420-480 mm. **Weight** 450-700 g. Males are heavier.

Petaurus breviceps

Petaurus australis

POSSUMS

Feathertail Glider   *Acrobates pygmaeus*

The Feathertail Glider is the smallest and most cryptic of the gliding possums. The size
of a mouse, it has a flattened, feather-like tail with long stiff hairs on each side, used
as a steering aerofoil and as an extra limb. A small, thick, gliding membrane
extends from the elbows to the knees. The feet have a powerful grip with sharp
claws, 2 opposing toes on the forefeet, opposing first toes on the hindfeet, and
finely-grooved pads enabling it to climb smooth surfaces. A double claw on the
fused second and third toes of the hindfeet is used for grooming. It has a brush-tipped tongue
for feeding on nectar and large, forward-pointing eyes. **Behaviour** Active mainly at night,
Feathertail Gliders are fast and agile, leaping through the tree canopy and gliding more than 20 m. They share
bulky, spherical nests of leaves, ferns and bark strips in tree hollows or crevices, huddling together in cold or wet
weather, and becoming torpid when food is scarce. Up to 40 individuals may live in the same tree hollow, although
groups of 5-6 are more common, with females tending to outnumber males. Females form matrilineal groups comprising mothers and their female offspring. Young males disperse at about 6 months of age, and males appear to be
solitary outside the breeding season. **Development** Females become sexually mature at about 6 months, while
males are sexually active between 7 and 18 months. They have a lifespan of 3-4 years. Births occur between April and
February in the south, and year-round in the north. Females mate immediately after the birth of the first litter, the
new embryo remaining dormant until the first litter is weaned, hence 2-3 litters may be raised in quick succession.
Litter size varies from 1-4, although 2-3 is more usual. Females have 4 teats in a forward-opening pouch where the
young remain for 60-65 days, staying in the nest until weaned and independent at 95-100 days. **Diet** Pollen, nectar,
insects, honeydew and manna. Sap is licked from gashes made by Sugar and Yellow-bellied Gliders. **Habitat** Wet
and dry sclerophyll forests and woodlands from sea level to above 1200 m. **Traces** Scats are small and mouse-like,
about 5 mm long and 1 mm across, composed of very fine particles. **Status** Probably secure; vulnerable to logging of
old, hollow trees and predation by Cats and Foxes. **Head-body** 60-80 mm. **Tail** 60-80 mm. **Weight** 10-17 g. Males are
heavier than females.

Striped Possum   *Dactylopsila trivirgata*

The Striped Possum is a shy and slightly-built arboreal marsupial with a variable pattern of black and white stripes from its nose to the base of its bushy tail, and a white
Y-shaped pattern on its forehead. The belly is white, the limbs black-striped, and
the tip of the pendulous, prehensile tail is often white. It has large rounded ears, a
large blunt head with long, sharp, lower incisor teeth and a long tongue. The
hindfeet are adapted for grasping branches and have an opposing first toe, while
the second and third are toes fused and have a double claw for grooming. The Striped Possum
has a larger brain for its size than any other marsupial, and an extremely long fourth finger with a powerful curved
claw. **Behaviour** Active mainly at night, Striped Possums spend up to 9 hours per night foraging in the trees and
investigating rotten logs for insects, exposed by biting into the bark with their bayonet-like lower incisors, and
extracted with their long tongue or fourth finger. They are extremely agile and fast, leaping through the tree canopy
in pursuit of rivals, and running along branches with a peculiar lizard-like gait, moving opposite front and rear legs
together. During the day they sleep in leaf-lined nests in the hollows of large trees or clumps of epiphytes, using
many different den sites spread over a home range of 5-22 ha. They are very noisy, making guttural shrieks when
mating, snorting, rustling through the foliage, tearing at the bark, and making loud chewing and slurping sounds
when feeding. When handled they emit a strong musky odour. **Development** Mating probably occurs year round
with a peak in June-July. Up to 2 young are born, naked and with their eyes closed. Newborn attach to the 2 teats in
the mother's well-developed, forward-opening pouch. **Diet** Mostly wood-boring insects and larvae, supplemented by
leaves, fruits, small vertebrates and honey. **Habitat** Tropical rainforests, gallery forests, vine forests and adjoining
woodlands. **Traces** Feeding scars on tree trunks. Scats disappear in leaf litter. **Status** Probably secure, but rare,
sparse and vulnerable to logging. **Head-body** 240-280 mm. **Tail** 310-394 mm. **Weight** 240-569 g.

Acrobates pygmaeus

Dactylopsila trivirgata

POSSUMS

Little Pygmy-possum

Cercartetus lepidus

The smallest of the possums, this tiny, mouse-sized arboreal marsupial is light grey-brown above and grey below with soft, dense fur. The head is cone-shaped with broad oval ears and large eyes. The strongly prehensile tail tapers from a season-ally fat base to a sparsely-furred, pointed tip. Little Pygmy-possums can be distinguished from mice by their grasping hindfeet which have an opposing first toe and a double claw on the fused second and third toes used for grooming.

Behaviour Active at night, Little Pygmy-possums are fast and agile climbers, using their tail as a fifth limb. They forage in the lower levels of the forest and in thick scrub, catching and manipulating insects and small lizards with their forepaws. They sleep in abandoned birds' nests or in roughly-constructed nests of grass, leaves or shredded bark in tree hollows, crevices, stumps, or dense ground cover. In cold conditions or when food is scarce they curl up in a tight ball and become torpid for up to 7 days, lowering their body temperature to conserve energy and surviving from fat stored in the tail. Little is known about their social life, although in Tasmania nests are usually occupied by 2 adults. **Development** Females become sexually mature in their first year and breed throughout the year on the mainland, and from September to February in Tasmania. Usually 3-4 young are born and attach to the 4 teats in the mother's shallow, forward-opening pouch. They vacate the pouch at about 6 weeks and are left in the nest while the mother forages, or cling to the her back if she changes nests. The young are weaned at about 7 weeks. **Diet** Insects and their larvae, spiders, pollen, nectar and small lizards. **Habitat** Semi-arid mallee scrub, shrublands, wet and dry sclerophyll forests and woodlands. **Traces** Scats are difficult to find, mouse-like, 2-3 mm long, comprising very fine particles of insects and pollen. **Status** Probably secure; vulnerable to changes in land use and fire regimes. **Head-body** 66-76 mm. **Tail** 60-75 mm. **Weight** 6-13 g.

Eastern Pygmy-possum

Cercartetus nanus

The size of a large mouse, this arboreal marsupial has soft dense fur, fawn-grey to olive-brown above and light-grey to white below. The rounded head has very large eyes and ears and long whiskers. The prehensile tail has a fat base in good seasons, is almost naked and tapers to a fine point. The first 2 toes of the hindfeet oppose the other 3, enabling it to grasp branches, while the second and third toes are fused with a double claw for grooming. **Behaviour** Solitary and docile, Eastern Pygmy-possums are predominantly nocturnal, although they sometimes emerge on overcast days. They occupy overlapping home ranges of about 0.7 ha for males and 0.34 ha for females, sheltering in tree hollows, stumps, under bark, in the forks of tea trees, in dense vegetation or disused bird nests. Several nests are used by individuals, and females may share them with their juvenile offspring. Pregnant and lactating females construct small spherical nests about 6 cm across of shredded bark lined with fresh leaves. They are largely arboreal, moving at a moderate pace among the foliage, sometimes suspended by their tail. In cold conditions they become torpid for up to 2 weeks, conserving energy and using fat reserves stored in the tail. When provoked they utter a loud hiss. **Development** Sexually mature at 4.5-9 months, they generally breed from spring to autumn on the mainland and in late winter and spring in Tasmania, giving birth to 2-4 young, raising 2-3 litters per season on the mainland in good years. Mating takes place soon after the birth of the first litter, although the embryo remains dormant until the pouch is empty. Young are born some 30 days after mating and attach to the 4 functional teats in the mother's shallow pouch (she usually has 6 teats). They leave the pouch after 33-37 days and suckle while clinging to the mother's belly fur. They are weaned at about 60-65 days, become independent immediately, and have a lifespan of 3-5 years. **Diet** Pollen and nectar gathered with the slightly brush-tipped tongue, insects, seeds and soft fruits. **Habitat** Wet sclerophyll forests, rainforests, heaths and shrublands, from sea level to about 1600 m. **Traces** Scats are about 5 mm long and 2 mm wide, comprising fine particles of pollen, seeds and insects. **Status** Secure. **Head-body** 70-110 mm. **Tail** 75-110 mm. **Weight** 15-45 g.

Cercartetus lepidus

Cercartetus nanus

Western Pygmy-possum

Cercartetus concinnus

The size of a large mouse, this arboreal marsupial is fawn to reddish-brown above with white belly fur. It has a conical head with large mobile ears, large eyes and very long whiskers. The tail is strongly prehensile and naked for most of its length with fine scales to give it extra grip. The tail tapers to a point from a seasonally-fattened base, and is coiled when not in use. Like the other possums the first toes of the hindfeet oppose the other 3, enabling it to grasp branches, while the second and third toes are fused with a double claw for grooming. **Behaviour** Active mainly at night, Western Pygmy-possums move quickly through the foliage, occasionally leaping between branches, using their tail as a fifth limb. They also forage on the ground, moving on all-fours and holding food in the forepaws. Solitary and cryptic, they sleep in disued bird nests, among ground litter, or in a spherical nest of shredded bark or leaves in a tree hollow, stump, or the crown of a grass tree. On cold or wet days they curl up into a tight ball and become torpid for periods of up to 11 days, lowering their body temperature and surviving on fat stored in the tail. **Development** Females are sexually mature at 12-15 months and breed throughout the year, producing 2-3 litters in close succession. Mating takes place soon after giving birth, although the resultant embryos remain dormant until the pouch is empty. No more than 6 young are reared. The newborn attach to the 6 teats in the mother's forward-opening pouch, where they remain for about 25 days. Blind and semi-furred, the young are left in the nest until weaned at about 50 days old. **Diet** Nectar, pollen, seeds, insects and perhaps small lizards. **Habitat** Dry sclerophyll forests and woodlands with a dense understorey, and semi-arid mallee scrub. **Traces** Scats are small and mouse-like, about 5 mm long, composed of very fine particles of pollen, seeds and insects. **Status** Endangered; threatened by land clearing and predation by Cats. **Head-body** 70-110 mm. **Tail** 70-96 mm. **Weight** 8-21 g.

Mountain Pygmy-possum

Burramys parvus

The only Australian mammal restricted to alpine and subalpine areas, the Mountain Pygmy-possum is a largely terrestrial, rat-sized marsupial. It has fine, dense fur, grey-brown above, sometimes darker along the mid-back, pale grey-brown to cream below, and darker around the eyes. It has a long, thin tail, covered with scales and sparse, fine hair. The hindfeet are capable of grasping with an opposing first toe, while the second and third toes are fused with a double claw used for grooming. **Behaviour** Active mainly at night, Mountain Pygmy-possums climb among rocks and shrubs looking for food, manipulating it with the hands while squatting. Seeds are stored in the nest, under bark or beneath loose soil. They sleep in nests of shredded bark, leaves or grass, carried in the curled tail and placed in rock crevices or among dense vegetation. Males and females share nests during the breeding season, but males are forced to disperse to poorer habitats on the periphery of the breeding areas when the young leave the pouch. Juvenile males are forced out after weaning, leaving females in the best habitat and 4-5 times more likely to survive over winter than males. Females occupy non-exclusive home ranges from 0.06-7.7 ha, while males range over large distances, often travelling 1.5 km overnight. They build up fat in summer and autumn, and hibernate for up to 7 months. **Development** Mountain Pygmy-possums breed in their first year of life, from late October to early December, usually producing more than 4 young, 13-16 days after mating. Only those able to attach to the 4 teats in the mother's forward-opening pouch survive. At about 30 days old they are deposited in the nest, and stay there until independent, 30-35 days later. The longest living of the small terrestrial mammals, females have a lifespan of more than 11 years in captivity and 5 years in the wild. **Diet** Moths and other invertebrates, fruits and seeds. **Habitat** Rock scree and boulder-fields in heaths, sedgelands, shrublands and woodlands above 1430 m. **Traces** Transversely cracked seeds of the mountain plum pine. Scats are small and mouse-like, about 5 mm long, containing fragments of seeds, berries and insects. **Status** Endangered; restricted to Mt Hotham and Kosciuszko areas; threatened by tourist development. **Head-body** 100-120 mm. **Tail** 130-160 mm. **Weight** 30-82 g.

Cercartetus concinnus

Burramys parvus

Honey Possum

Tarsipes rostratus

This mouse-size arboreal marsupial has a very long snout and a long, brush-tipped tongue. It has coarse fur, grizzled greyish-brown above and cream below with 3 dark stripes along the back. The eyes are near the top of the head, the ears are rounded and the tail is long, thin, strongly prehensile and sparsely furred. The teeth are rudimentary pegs except for 2 long, pointed, lower incisors. The hands and feet have opposing first digits and large rough pads for gripping branches, the second and third toes of the hindfeet are fused and used for grooming; the claws are reduced to small nails. **Behaviour** Active mainly at night, Honey Possums are very fast moving and agile, darting between blossoms, extracting pollen and nectar with their long, brush-tipped tongue. They run on all-fours with the tail held straight out behind, and can walk below branches and climb vertically. They live in overlapping home ranges of about 1 ha and sleep during the day. They do not build nests, but shelter in the hollow stems of grass trees or abandoned bird nests, sometimes sharing sites. On cold days they huddle together for warmth and become torpid for short periods to save energy when food is short. Females are dominant to males, and several males may compete to mate with a female. **Development** Sexually mature at about 6 months, with a life expectancy of 1-2 years, they breed throughout the year with peaks in early autumn, winter and spring when food is most abundant, producing 2-3 litters per year. Up to 4 young are born 21-28 days after mating. Newborn weigh about 5 mg and are the smallest mammalian young. They attach to the 4 teats in the mother's forward-opening pouch, emerging at about 65 days, when they are left in a shelter or nest while the mother forages. The young disperse after weaning at 90 days. Females carry quiescent embryos which develop when the pouch is empty. **Diet** Pollen and nectar. **Habitat** Sandplain heaths and shrublands with nectar-producing plants (notably Proteaceae and Myrtaceae families). **Status** Probably secure; vulnerable to Fox and Cat predation and land clearing. **Head-body** 40-95 mm. **Tail** 45-110 mm. **Weight** 7-12 g. Females are usually larger than males.

Long-tailed Pygmy-possum

Cercartetus caudatus

The size of a large mouse, this arboreal marsupial is brownish-grey above with a distinct dark eye patch, and pale-grey below. It has a long, thin prehensile tail with a furry, slightly thickened base. The head has a narrow, pointed muzzle with a pink nose, large eyes and large thin ears. The first toe of the hindfoot is short and clawless with a bulbous tip and opposes the others for gripping branches. The second and third toes are fused with a double claw for grooming. **Behaviour** Active at night, Long-tailed Pygmy-possums sleep in spherical nests of leaves or fern fronds in hollows in trees, stumps, or in fern clumps. They are cryptic in their habits, and usually forage alone, although groups of up to 4 have been seen feeding together. Lactating females may share nests with their offspring, and adult males sometimes share nests, occasionally with a female. On cool winter days when food is scarce they become torpid to conserve energy. They are agile climbers, using their long, prehensile tail as a fifth limb. When threatened they utter a throaty roar or a quiet defensive hiss. **Development** Sexually mature at 15 months, Long-tailed Pygmy-possums mate in January and February and from late August to early November, producing up to 4 young per litter. Newborn each attach to the 4 teats in the mother's forward-opening pouch, which they vacate at about 45 days when they weigh 5-7 g. Young are weaned at about 80 days and become independent at 90 days. **Diet** Nectar and insects. **Habitat** Tropical rainforests and open forests fringing rainforests. **Status** Probably secure; vulnerable to logging. **Head-body** 100-110 mm. **Tail** 125-151 mm. **Weight** 20-40 g.

Tarsipes rostratus

Cercartetus caudatus

Long-nosed Potoroo

Potorous tridactylus

This squat, Rabbit-size, kangaroo-like marsupial has a prehensile tail used to gather nesting material, well-developed upper canine teeth and upper and lower incisor teeth that bite against each other. The fur is grey to brown above (dark rufous-brown in Tasmania) and paler below. It has a long, tapering nose with a naked tip, rounded ears and a scaly tail with a furry base. The forelimbs are short and muscular with forward-pointing toes with spatulate claws used to dig for food. The second and third toes of the hindfeet are short and fused with a double claw used for grooming, the fourth toe is long and the fifth short. **Behaviour** Long-nosed potoroos forage on the forest floor between dusk and dawn, moving slowly with a short hop, smelling out underground fungi which are dug up with the forefeet. If disturbed they leap quickly away on their hind legs, using their forelimbs to change direction. They sleep by day in simple nests of grass and other vegetation carried in the curled tail and placed in scrapes below dense scrub, grass tussocks or grass trees. In bush fires they seek refuge in the burrows of other animals. Solitary and sedentary except when mating, they have overlapping home ranges of up to 10 ha, rarely venture far from cover and sometimes gather in small groups. **Development** Sexually mature at 12 months, Long-nosed potoroos have a life expectancy of around 4-7 years in the wild, and breed year-round with peaks in summer and late winter. A single young is born 38 days after mating and attaches firmly to one of 4 teats in the mother's pouch, leaving the pouch by 15 weeks and suckling at foot for 5-6 weeks. Mating may occur soon after birth, but the embryo remains dormant until the pouch is empty. **Diet** Mostly fungi, supplemented by insects, roots, seeds and fruit. **Habitat** Coastal heaths, rainforests, sclerophyll forests and woodlands with a dense understorey, to 1600 m. **Traces** Cone-shaped diggings up to 25 cm deep. Scats are deposited near feeding sites. They are oval to cylindrical, 5-10 mm across, comprising fine particles of soil, spores and plant material. **Status** Probably secure; sparsely distributed; vulnerable in NSW; threatened by land clearing. **Head-body** 320-400 mm. **Tail** 195-265 mm. **Weight** 660-2070 g. Males are larger than females.

Musky Rat-kangaroo

Hypsiprymnodon moschatus

This rat-size marsupial is the smallest macropod and the only one with an opposing, clawless first toe on the hindfoot, enabling it to climb and grip branches. The fur is dense and soft, rich rufous-brown flecked with darker hairs above, paler below with patches of white to cream on the throat and chest. The tail is relatively short, dark-brown with small non-overlapping scales. The head is long and slender with large rounded ears and a naked nose. The hindfeet are relatively short with 5 toes, sharp curved claws and striated pads on the palms and soles; the second and third toes are fused at the base. **Behaviour** Active during the day, they forage in the early morning and late afternoon on the forest floor and along creek banks. They sleep at midday and during the night in nests of dried grass, ferns and lichen carried in the curled tail and built in clumps of lawyer vines, beneath tree buttresses or in rock piles. Individuals use several nests and females construct much larger maternity nests. They are solitary with small home ranges, but sometimes feed with up to 7 others. They climb among fallen trees and branches and move with a slow hop on the ground with the tail held out behind, or run with a galloping gait, the hindfeet moving forward outside the forelimbs. Courtship includes standing erect, face-to-face, touching the partner's head and neck with the forepaws, and precedes mating by several days. **Development** Sexually mature at about 2 years, they mate from October to April and usually give birth to 1-3 young. Newborn attach firmly to the 4 teats in the mother's pouch. They vacate the pouch about 21 weeks later and spend several more weeks in the nest before accompanying the mother to feed. **Diet** Insects, small animals, fungi, fruits and large seeds manipulated with the forepaws. **Habitat** Tropical rainforests near creeks, to 1500 m. **Traces** Scats are dark-brown to black, roughly cylindrical, about 5 mm across and 5-20 mm long, containing fine fibrous particles and some insect remains. **Status** Vulnerable; threatened by rainforest clearing. **Head-body** 153-307 mm. **Tail** 123-165 mm. **Weight** 337-680 g.

Potorous tridactylus

Hypsiprymnodon moschatus

Brush-tailed Bettong

Bettongia penicillata

Also known as the Woylie, this squat, Rabbit-size, kangaroo-like marsupial has a pre-hensile tail used to gather nesting material, well-developed upper canine teeth and upper and lower incisor teeth that bite against each other. It is sandy-brown to yellow-grey flecked with white above, and pale grey-brown to white below, with a black bushy tail tip. It has a broad head with a flattened, naked nose and pointed ears. The short, muscular forelimbs have forward-pointing toes with spatu-late claws used for digging. The hindfeet have no first digit, the second and third are fused with a double claw used for grooming, and the fourth is much longer than the others. **Behaviour** Brush-tailed Bettongs for-age at night, digging in the soil and leaf litter for food, hopping away quickly if disturbed with the head low, the back arched and the tail held out straight behind. They sleep in well-concealed domed nests about 20 cm across, made from shredded bark lined with grass. The nests are built over shallow depressions dug beneath shrubs or other cover. They are solitary except during the breeding season, and utilise large home ranges of 20 ha or more, incorpo-rating several nests and a feeding area sometimes shared with neighbouring Bettongs. **Development** Female Brush-tailed Bettongs are sexually mature at 5-6 months, males at 9-12 months, with a life expectancy of 4-6 years. They breed year round and produce 2-3 litters per year. Mating occurs soon after birth, although the embryo remains dormant until the pouch is empty. After a pregnancy of 21 days the newborn attaches to one of 4 teats in the mother's pouch, which it vacates at about 14 weeks, suckling at foot for another 60-70 days and sharing the mother's nest until the next young leaves the pouch. **Diet** Underground fungi, bulbs, tubers, seeds, gum exudate and insects. They can survive without drinking. **Habitat** Dry sclerophyll forests and woodlands with good ground cover, to about 300 m. **Traces** Small, cone-shaped diggings. Scats are oval to cylindrical, about 8 mm across and 10-20 mm long, con-taining fine soil particles and fungal spores. **Status** Endangered; threatened by land clearing and Fox predation. **Head-body** 300-380 mm. **Tail** 290-360 mm. **Weight** 1.1-1.6 kg.

Rufous Bettong

Aepyprymnus rufescens

The largest bettong, distinguished by its hairy muzzle, the Rufous Bettong is reddish-brown to grey-brown flecked with light-grey above, and white below. Like the other bettongs it has a very long fourth toe on its hindfoot and a double claw on its fused second and third toes for grooming. It has long, curved claws on its forefeet for digging, and uses its prehensile tail to carry nesting material. **Behaviour** Rufous Bettongs forage on the forest floor at night, digging holes with their forefeet, and often feeding in small groups. When alarmed they stand upright, hold their arms stiffly by their sides, stamp their hindfeet and hop quickly away, forelegs tucked against their sides. They sleep in spherical to cone-shaped nests made of grass collected in the mouth and carried in the curled-up tail. Clusters of nests are built, often close to a feeding site, they have a single entrance and are constructed over shallow scrapes at the base of grass tussocks, under logs or rocks. Individuals may travel 4.5 km overnight and use up to 5 nests at any one time, abandoning them every month or so. Males have home ranges of 75-110 ha and females 45-60 ha. Their home ranges overlap, and males often associate exclusively with 1-2 females. Vocalisations include growls, grunts and low, warning hisses. **Development** Sexually mature at 11-12 months, they breed throughout the year and females mate soon after giving birth, although the embryo remains dormant until the pouch is vacated. After a pregnancy of 22-24 days a single young is born, probably in the nest, and attaches to one of 4 teats in the mother's pouch for 7-8 weeks. The pouch is vacated at 14-16 weeks and the young suckles at foot for another 7 weeks. **Diet** Tubers, roots, herbs, fungi, insects, seeds, tree exudates and flowers. They can survive without drinking, except in droughts. **Habitat** Open forests and woodlands with a sparse or grassy understorey, to 1000 m. **Traces** Small con-ical diggings over large areas. Scats are oval, about 10 mm across and 10-20 mm long, containing coarse plant mate-rial. **Status** Vulnerable; threatened by land clearing, competition from Rabbits and Fox predation. **Head-body** 370-390 mm. **Tail** 335-390 mm. **Weight** to 3.5 kg. Females are larger than males.

Bettongia penicillata

Aepyprymnus rufescens

Tasmanian Bettong

Bettongia gaimardi

The Tasmanian Bettong is now extinct on the mainland, but is still widespread in
Tasmania where there are no Foxes. It has a prehensile tail used to carry nesting
material, well-developed upper canine teeth, and upper and lower incisor teeth
that bite against each other. The broad head has rounded ears and a naked nose.
The fur is coarse with soft underfur, brownish-grey flecked with dark-brown to
black above, and greyish-white below. The tail is well-furred, dark-brown towards
the end with a white tip. The short muscular forelimbs have forward-pointing toes with long,
curved claws for digging. The hindfeet have no first digit, the second and third are fused with a double
claw used for grooming, while the fourth toe is much longer than the others. **Behaviour** Nocturnal and usually solitary, Tasmanian Bettongs have large home ranges of 65-135 ha, and travel more than 1 km to feeding sites, where
they sniff out and dig up underground fungi. They sleep by day in ovoid nests about 300 mm long and 200 mm wide
with a small entrance, built from densely-woven dry grass and bark strips carried in the curled tail and manipulated with the snout. Nests are constructed over shallow depressions dug beneath shrubs, grass tussocks or logs. A
nest may be used for a month or more and then abandoned for a similar period before being reoccupied. They have
anal scent-producing glands, probably used to mark the nest site. **Development** Sexually mature at 8-12 months,
Tasmanian Bettongs breed throughout the year. Females mate soon after giving birth, although the embryo remains
dormant until the pouch is vacated. After a pregnancy of 21-22 days a single young is born and attaches to one of 4
teats in the mother's pouch. The pouch is vacated at 14-16 weeks and the young suckles at foot for a further 7-8
weeks. **Diet** Mostly underground fungi, with some seeds, fruits, roots and bulbs. **Habitat** Dry sclerophyll forests
with open grassy understorey, to more than 1000 m, with an annual rainfall of 500-750 mm. **Traces** Small conical
diggings and oval scats about 10 mm across and 10-20 mm long, containing fine soil particles. **Status** Vulnerable;
threatened by habitat loss, competition from Rabbits and predation by Cats and Dogs. **Head-body** 310-350 mm.
Tail 285-350 mm. **Weight** 1.2-2.3 kg.

Spectacled Hare-wallaby

Lagorchestes conspicillatus

The Spectacled Hare-wallaby is a stout, short-necked marsupial of the tropical
grasslands, and derives its name from the rufous-brown rings surrounding its
eyes. It is brown flecked with white above, and white below, with white stripes on
the hips. The tail is sparsely-haired and darker towards the tip. The face is
square viewed from the front, with a black nose and pointed ears. The long hindfeet have no first toe, the second and third are fused with a double claw used for
grooming, and the fourth toe is much longer than the others. **Behaviour** Spectacled Hare-
wallabies are nocturnal and generally solitary, emerging at night to graze, and sometimes feeding with
1-2 others. They shelter from the daytime heat in cool hides tunnelled into grass tussocks, spinifex hummocks, or
formed in clumps of porcupine grass. Several hides are used in a home range of 8-10 ha. They are powerful jumpers
are move with a fast, hopping gait. Vocalisations include a soft clicking sound and a warning hiss. They conserve
water in hot dry conditions by raising their body temperature and eating less food, hence reducing the amount of
water needed for cooling and digestion. **Development** Sexually mature at 12 months, Spectacled Hare-wallabies
breed year-round, with peaks in March and September on Barrow Island. A single young is born 29-31 days after
mating and attaches firmly to one of the 4 teats in the mother's pouch. The pouch is vacated at about 5 months.
Mating takes place soon after giving birth, although development of the embryo is delayed until the pouch is empty,
or in drought conditions until food is more plentiful. **Diet** Leaves and native grasses. **Habitat** Tropical grasslands,
open forests, woodlands and shrublands. **Traces** Scats are slightly flattened, dark-brown, oval to oblong pellets,
about 10 mm across and 10-20 mm long, containing fairly coarse plant fragments, usually found in groups of about
4-8. **Status** Vulnerable; threatened by Fox and Cat predation and habitat degradation. **Head-body** 400-470 mm.
Tail 370-490 mm. **Weight** 1.6-4.5 kg.

Bettongia gaimardi

Lagorchestes conspicillatus

Black-footed Rock-wallaby

Petrogale lateralis

Found in arid and semi-arid areas of central and western Australia, the Black-footed Rock-wallaby is a widespread species with scattered populations comprising 6 chromosomally distinct forms. It has thick, soft fur, reddish-brown to purple above, pale yellow-brown below, grey to purple on the neck and shoulders, with a black stripe from the back of the head to the mid-back, and sometimes with white cheek and side stripes. The feet are dark-brown and the tail has a dark-brown to black tip. The hindfeet have no first digit, the second and third are fused with a double claw used for grooming, and the claw of the long fourth toe projects only slightly beyond the large pad. The pads are granulated with a fringe of stiff hairs. **Behaviour** Black-footed Rock-wallabies are predominantly nocturnal, sheltering in caves and rocky crevices from the heat of the day. They emerge in the late afternoon or evening to feed, and on cool days often bask in the sun. They are gregarious and live in colonies with separate male and female dominance hierarchies, established mainly by ritualised and aggressive acts, including kicking, but rarely actually fighting. They hop with great agility on rocky outcrops with the tail arched over the back. **Development** Females are sexually mature at 12-24 months and mate soon after giving birth to a single young, although development of the embryo is delayed until the pouch is vacated. The newborn attaches firmly to one of 4 teats in the mother's pouch. **Diet** Grasses and other vegetable matter. **Habitat** Semi-arid to arid rocky granite outcrops with mallee and other scrub and tussock grassland, often in montane areas. **Status** Probably secure, but declining in some areas; vulnerable to Fox predation and competition from Rabbits. **Head-body** 445-610 mm. **Tail** 320-610 mm. **Weight** 2.3-7.1 kg.

Brush-tailed Rock-wallaby

Petrogale penicillata

The Brush-tailed Rock-wallaby has a dull-brown back, a rufous rump, black furry feet and a long, densely-furred tail with a bushy tip. Southern animals are more colourful with a black tail and armpits, pale stripes along the sides, white cheek stripes, a black stripe on the forehead, and ears with black patches, whitish margins and yellowish inside. The hindfeet have no first digit, the second and third are fused with a double claw used for grooming, and the claw of the long fourth toe projects only slightly beyond the large pad. The pads are granulated for gripping, with a fringe of stiff hairs. **Behaviour** Brush-tailed Rock-wallabies are nocturnal, sheltering by day in caves, rocky crevices and dense stands of lantana. They form small colonies with dominance hierarchies, although individuals have overlapping home ranges of around 15 ha with exclusive den sites. Females are gregarious and frequently share den sites with female relatives and groom each other regularly. They hop with great agility on rocky outcrops with the tail arched over the back, and can ascend almost vertical rock faces and climb sloping tree trunks. Young at foot are left in the den while the mother looks for food or drink, often travelling long distances. **Development** Females are sexual mature by 18 months, males by 20 months. They breed all year, mating soon after giving birth, although development of the embryo is delayed until the pouch is vacated. After a pregnancy of 31 days a single young is born and attaches to one of 4 teats in the pouch, where it remains for about 29 weeks, thereafter suckling at foot for about 3 months. **Diet** Mainly grasses, supplemented with leaves, sedges, ferns, roots, bark, fruit, seeds and flowers. **Habitat** Rock faces with large tumbled boulders, ledges and caves, close to grassy ares, often in open forests. **Traces** Scats are found in groups of 4-8 near rock shelters and feeding sites. They are cylindrical pellets 10 mm or more across and 15-30 mm long, usually brown with coarse plant fragments. **Status** Vulnerable; endangered in NSW and Vic.; threatened by Fox predation and competition from Goats, Sheep and Rabbits. **Head-body** 450-586 mm. **Tail** 510-700 mm. **Weight** 4-10.9 kg. Males are larger than females.

Petrogale lateralis

Petrogale penicillata

Short-eared Rock-wallaby

Petrogale brachyotis

Although abundant and distributed over a wide area, little is known about the biology of the Short-eared Rock-wallaby. The fur is short and fine, light grey above and white to greyish-white below. It has a dark-brown neck stripe, a white shoulder patch and a dark tip to the tail. Arnhem Land individuals are dark-grey to brown above with a distinct white or buff side stripe, a dark neck and back stripe. The ears are less than half the length of the head and have a whitish margin. The hind-feet have no first digit, the second and third are fused with a double claw used for grooming, and the fourth is much longer than the others. **Behaviour** Short-eared Rock-wallabies are nocturnal, and sleep by day in cool rocky crevices or among boulders. They emerge in the evening to feed in adjacent areas, often with others. **Development** They probably breed throughout the year with a peak in the wet season, giving birth to a single young which attaches to one of the 4 teats in the mother's pouch. **Diet** Predominantly leaves and seeds supplemented with a small amount of grass. **Habitat** Savanna grasslands, open forests and scrub on low rocky hills, cliffs and gorges. **Status** Probably secure. **Head-body** 405-550 mm. **Tail** 320-550 mm. **Weight** 2.2-5.6 kg. Males are larger than females.

Yellow-footed Rock-wallaby

Petrogale xanthopus

A very attractively ornamented and brightly-coloured species, the Yellow-footed Rock-wallaby is greyish-fawn above with rich brown stripes along the centre of the back, hips and arms, white stripes along the cheeks and sides, rufous-brown arms and legs, white underparts, and a rufous-brown tail with dark bands. The ears are long and the nose naked. The hindfeet have no first digit, the second and third are fused with a double claw used for grooming, and the fourth is much longer than the others. The claw of the fourth toe projects only slightly beyond the large pad. The pads are granulated for gripping, with a fringe of stiff hairs around them. **Behaviour** Active mainly at night, Yellow-footed Rock-wallabies bask in the sun in winter and shelter during the day under rocky outcrops or among vegetation between boulders, emerging in the evening to feed. They are gregarious, forming colonies of up to 100 individuals each with overlapping home ranges of 150-200 ha. Each rockpile within the colony's boundary is occupied by a group of females, a large male and several smaller males. Males establish dominance hierarchies by ritualised aggressive acts and occasionally fighting. They are agile, hopping among rocks with the tail arched over the back, and are able to climb sloping tree trunks. The young are left behind in a safe place while the mother forages for food or drink, often travelling long distances. The young make a clicking call when lost or disturbed.

Development Females reach sexual maturity between 11 and 22 months, males at about 30 months. They are able to breed throughout the year and mate soon after giving birth, although development of the embryo is delayed until the pouch is vacated. After a pregnancy of 31-32 days a single young is born and attaches to one of the 4 teats in the mother's pouch, where it remains for about 28 weeks, thereafter suckling at foot until weaned. **Diet** Foliage supplemented with grass, herbs, tubers and bark. They need access to water and drink frequently in hot weather.
Habitat Semi-arid rocky sites with open woodland and scrub. **Traces** Scats are deposited in groups around rockpiles. They are cylindrical to oval, 10-15 mm across and 20-30 mm long, comprising coarse plant fragments.
Status Endangered; threatened by competition from Goats, habitat destruction, and predation by Cats and Foxes.
Head-body 480-650 mm. **Tail** 560-700 mm. **Weight** 6-12 kg. Males are larger than females.

Petrogale brachyotis

Petrogale xanthopus

Red-legged Pademelon

Thylogale stigmatica

A small, compact macropod generally found in rainforests and other densely-vege-
tated habitats, the Red-legged Pademelon has thick soft fur, grey-brown to dark-
brown above with red-brown markings on the cheeks, thighs and forearms. The
ears are rounded, the nose naked and the tail short and thick. The hindfeet have
no first digit, the second and third are fused with a double claw used for grooming, and the fourth is much longer than the others. **Behaviour** Red-legged
Pademelons are active most of the day and night, although they usually rest between midday
and early afternoon and around midnight. Daylight hours are spent searching for food within the forest, foraging on the ground and moving slowly with on all-fours. After dusk they follow well-defined runways through
the vegetation to feeding sites on the forest edge. They sleep in refuges in dense cover, sitting with the tail between
the legs, leaning back on a rock or tree and sleeping with the head on the tail or ground. Shy and generally solitary,
they have home ranges of 1-4 ha, and rarely venture more than 70 m from the forest edge. They sometimes feed in
small groups and when disturbed they thump the ground with the hindfeet as they dash for cover. Vocalisations
include a soft clucking by females calling their young and by males during courtship; and a harsh rasp made by
females in hostile situations or when rejecting courtship advances by a male. **Development** Males and females
become sexually mature at about 66 weeks and 48 weeks respectively. Females give birth to a single young 28-30
days after mating, and mate again 2-12 hours later, although development of the embryo is delayed until the pouch is
empty. The newborn attaches to one of 4 teats in the mother's well-developed pouch, detaching at 13-18 weeks,
opening its eyes at 16-18 weeks and making short excursions from the pouch at 22-26 weeks. Young vacate the pouch
at 26-18 weeks and are weaned 9-10 weeks later. **Diet** Leaves, fruit, ferns, fungi and grasses. **Habitat** Rainforests,
wet sclerophyll forests and vine scrubs. **Traces** Small resting hollows and well-worn runways in dense vegetation.
Scats are about 1 cm across and 2 cm long, black or brown, containing coarse plant fragments. **Status** Secure.
Head-body 385-540 mm. **Tail** 300-475 mm. **Weight** 2.5-6.8 kg. Males are larger than females.

Red-necked Pademelon

Thylogale thetis

The Red-necked Pademelon is a compact macropod of the forest edge, distinguished
from the Red-legged Pademelon by the reddish-brown fur around its neck and
shoulders. The fur is thick and soft, brownish-grey above and whitish below. The
ears are rounded, the nose naked and the tail short and thick. The hindfeet have
no first digit, the second and third are fused with a double claw used for grooming, and the fourth is much longer than the others. **Behaviour** Active most of the
day, Red-necked Pademelons move slowly through the forest in daylight hours between bouts
of sleep, seeking food, and basking in the sun in winter. After dusk they travel along well-defined runways
to forest clearings and feeding sites at forest edge, returning to cover just before dawn. They sleep in dense cover in
shallow depressions in the leaf litter. Shy and generally solitary, they have home ranges of 5-30 ha and rarely venture
more than 100 m from the forest edge. Small feeding groups often congregate in clearings at night, hopping quickly
back to cover if disturbed with the tail held out stiffly behind. Slow movements are quadrupedal with the tail dragging behind. Vocalisations include a threatening growl, a repetitive click by females calling their young and a clucking sound made by males during courtship. If alarmed they thump their hindfeet as they hop away. Males establish
dominance hierarchies by fighting or ritualised aggression. **Development** Sexually mature at 17 months, they breed
all year with birth peaks in autumn and spring in northern areas and January-February in the south. A single young
is born and attaches to one of the 4 teats in the mother's pouch, vacating the pouch by 26 weeks and suckling at foot
for a further 4 weeks. **Diet** Grasses, herbs and leaves, often holding food in the forepaws. **Habitat** Margins of closed
forests and rainforests. **Traces** Similar to the Red-legged Pademelon. **Status** Secure. **Head-body** 290-620 mm.
Tail 270-510 mm. **Weight** 1.8-9.2 kg. Males are larger than females.

Thylogale stigmatica

Thylogale thetis

Quokka

Setonix brachyurus

The Quokka is a small, robust wallaby with long, thick, coarse fur flecked with grey and brown, tinged rufous on the back and pale grey below. The head is broad with a dark stripe on the forehead and small rounded ears set on top. The tail is thick and sparsely-haired with visible scales. The hindfeet have no first digit, the second and third are fused with a double claw used for grooming, and the fourth is much longer than the others. **Behaviour** Active mainly at night, Quokkas shelter by day in groups in dense vegetation and converge at night around waterholes within a group territory occupied and defended by 25-150 adults. In dry conditions adults sometimes fight for available shelter and water. They live in overlapping home ranges of around 4 ha and adult males establish dominance hierarchies according to age. Females and juveniles have no rank in the hierarchy. Males defend areas around their resting sites and may form long term bonds with females. They move with a bounding gait interspersed with short bouts of rapid hopping, and may climb trees to reach twigs up to 2 m above ground. **Development** Quokkas have a life span of 10 years or more. Females are sexually mature at 18-24 months and breed throughout the year on the mainland. On Rottnest Island, however, breeding takes place from January to August. After a pregnancy of 25-28 days a single young is born and attaches to one of 4 teats in the mother's pouch. The young vacates the pouch by 26 weeks and suckles at foot for 2 months. **Diet** Grasses, leaves and succulents. They can survive for long periods without water and have been observed drinking seawater. **Habitat** Wet and dry sclerophyll forests, woodlands and heath. **Traces** Scats are found in groups at feeding sites and resting places. They are oval to oblong, about 15 mm across and 15-25 mm long, containing coarse plant fragments. **Status** Vulnerable; threatened by land clearing and Fox predation. **Head-body** 400-540 mm. **Tail** 245-310 mm. **Weight** 2.4-4.2 kg.

Tasmanian Pademelon

Thylogale billardierii

A small, stockily-built macropod, the Tasmanian Pademelon has long, dense and soft fur, dark-brown to golden-brown above with a grey base, and pale reddish-buff below with a grey to white base. The tail is short and thick, the ears rounded and the nose naked. The hindfeet have no first digit, the second and third are fused with a double claw used for grooming, and the fourth is much longer than the others. **Behaviour** Tasmanian Pademelons are generally active from dusk to dawn and rarely venture more than 100 m from the forest edge. They sleep by day in dense cover, although in winter and when the weather is bad they emerge to feed during the day, digging food from the snow in alpine areas. They are basically solitary with home ranges as large as 170 ha, and travel along well-established runways to feeding sites up to 2 km away where they congregate in groups of 10 or more. They have a short rapid hop and escape to dense undergrowth when alarmed. Males establish dominance hierarchies during the breeding season by fighting and ritualised aggression. Top-ranking males have exclusive mating rights with females. Males utter a guttural growl or hiss when fighting and make clucking sounds during courtship. **Development** Tasmanian Pademelons are sexually mature at about 14 months, and although capable of breeding year round, most births occur from April to June. Females mate within 24 hours of giving birth, but the embryo remains dormant until the pouch is empty. After a pregnancy of 30 days a single young is born and attaches to one of the 4 teats in the mother's pouch. The infant leaves the pouch at about 29 weeks and suckles at foot until about 10 months old. **Diet** Soft grasses, herbs, leaves and seedlings, often held in the forepaws. **Habitat** Coastal and montane forests and scrubs with dense undergrowth and adjacent grassy areas. **Traces** Small resting hollows in dense vegetation and well-worn runways. Scats are oval to cylindrical, about 10-15 mm across and 15-25 mm long, brown, containing coarse plant fragments. **Status** Secure. **Head-body** 360-720 mm. **Tail** 320-485 mm. **Weight** 2.4-12 kg. Males are much larger than females.

Setonix brachyurus

Thylogale billardierii

Lumholtz's Tree-kangaroo

Dendrolagus lumholtzi

Found in the rainforests of northeastern Australia, this unusual kangaroo varies in colour from pale creamy-brown to grey or rusty-brown with lighter flecks on the rump. It has black paws and a pale band across the forehead and down the sides of the face. The ears are very small and rounded and the tail is long and thick but not prehensile. It has shorter limbs than the ground-dwelling kangaroos with stout, muscular forelimbs armed with strong, sharp, curved claws to help it climb. The toes on the hindfeet are all about the same length with uniformly granular soles for extra grip and strong, curved claws. A double claw on the second and third fused toes is used for grooming.

Behaviour Lumholtz's Tree-kangaroos are nocturnal, sleeping by day crouched on a branch in the crown of a tree, often in the sun. They feed in the mid-level of the canopy and understorey, climbing with the tail hanging loosely, gripping with their clawed forefeet and balancing with the hindfeet. They move forwards or backwards with alternate movements of the hindlegs, hop along broad branches and jump from tree to tree, crashing through the canopy. They descend backwards and can jump 10 m or more to the ground, landing on their feet. On the ground they walk or run quadrupedally and hop with the forelegs tucked into the body and the tail held out stiffly. Usually solitary, they occupy small overlapping home ranges of about 0.7 ha for females and 1.8 ha for males, and sometimes feed in groups of 2-4. Juvenile males are probably evicted from the mother's home range and forced to disperse. Males are very aggressive to each other, and can inflict fatal wounds with their claws. During courtship the males make a soft clucking sound and gently paw the female's head and shoulders. **Development** Breeding probably takes place year round and females give birth to a single young which attaches to one of 4 teats in the mother's pouch. Pouch life is thought to be about 230 days, with the young staying at heel for up to 2 years. **Diet** Leaves supplemented by fruits and flowers. **Habitat** Tropical rainforests and associated wet sclerophyll forests. **Traces** Ruby-red eyeshine at night. Deep scratches on tree trunks. Distinctive musky odour. Scats are sometimes deposited on rocks. They are about 10 mm across and 10-25 mm long, containing coarse plant fragments. **Status** Vulnerable; threatened by logging, land clearing and feral Dogs. **Head-body** 480-650 mm. **Tail** 600-740 mm. **Weight** 3.7-10 kg. Males are larger than females.

Bennett's Tree-kangaroo

Dendrolagus bennettianus

Similar in many respects to Lumholtz's Tree-kangaroo, this arboreal marsupial of the rainforests of northeastern Australia is dark-brown above and light-fawn below with a rusty-brown area on the back of the head and shoulders. The forehead and muzzle are greyish, the feet, hands and base of the tail are black, the long tail has a bushy tip and a light-brown patch on the upper surface. The ears are small and rounded. It has stout, muscular forelimbs and relatively short hindfeet with toes all about the same length and granular soles. The claws are strong and curved. The second and third toes of the hindfeet are fused with a double claw used for grooming. **Behaviour** Predominantly nocturnal, Bennett's Tree-kangaroos spend most of the day sitting high up in the canopy, often basking in the sun in winter, hidden from view by vines and vegetation, and sleeping crouched on a branch. Wary and cryptic, they climb through the canopy at night, gripping branches with their clawed forefeet and balancing with the hindfeet. On the ground they walk or run quadrupedally or hop rapidly, and often travel long distances. Adults defend a discrete home range and males often fight. Male home ranges may be up to 25 ha and often overlap those of several females. Family groups of male, female and young at foot often feed in close proximity at night. They growl when alarmed and females call their young with soft trumpeting sounds. **Development** Details of their development are not known. They probably breed all year and give birth to a single young which attaches to one of the 4 teats in the mother's pouch. Young accompany the mother for up to 2 years. **Diet** Leaves supplemented by fruits. **Habitat** Tropical rainforests and vine forests. **Status** Vulnerable; threatened by logging and land clearing. **Head-body** 690-750 mm. **Tail** 730-840 mm. **Weight** 8-13.7 kg. Males are much larger than females.

Dendrolagus lumholtzi

Dendrolagus bennettianus

Northern Nailtail Wallaby

Onychogalea unguifera

The Northern Nailtail Wallaby derives its name from a small horny spur of unknown function hidden among a brush of dark hairs at the tip of its slender, whip-like tail. It is a small, sandy wallaby with a dark stripe along the lower back and tail, and a faint dark shoulder stripe. It has a squarish muzzle, long ears and very slender upper incisor teeth inclined forward. The forefeet have long, well developed claws used to dig shallow scrapes in the soil. The long hindfeet have no first digit, the second and third are fused with a double claw for grooming, and the fourth is much longer than the others. **Behaviour** Active between dusk and dawn, Northern Nailtail Wallabies rest by day in a shallow scrape in the shade under low trees, dense shrubs or grassy tussocks. They are usually solitary, but sometimes feed with 1-3 others, often travelling more than 3 km from daytime resting sites to feeding areas, always staying close to shelter. They move with a low, crouching hop with the tail curved upwards, but when travelling fast they move their forelimbs in an unusual rotary action, once likened to that of an organ-grinder. **Development** Little is known about their development. Females give birth to a single young which attaches firmly to one of 4 teats in the mother's pouch. **Diet** Herbs, leaves, native grasses, fruits, stem bases and rhizomes. **Habitat** Open grassy woodlands, tall shrublands, tussock grasslands and shrubby savanna, usually near water. **Traces** Scats are oval pellets about 10 mm across and 15-25 mm long, containing coarse plant fragments. **Status** Probably secure.
Head-body 490-690 mm. **Tail** 600-730 mm. **Weight** 4.5-9 kg. Males are larger than females.

Antilopine Wallaroo

Macropus antilopinus

A large marsupial of the tropical northern woodlands, the Antilopine Wallaroo resembles the Grey Kangaroos in appearance and behaviour, and derives its name from its long, fine, supposedly antelope-like fur. It is reddish sandy-brown above and very pale brown to white below, often with pale patches on the legs and tail. Females may be bluish-grey. The paws are black, the nose is naked and the tail relatively short and thick. The hindfeet have no first digit, the second and third are fused with a double claw for grooming, and the fourth is much longer than the others.
Behaviour Antilopine Wallaroos are generally active at night, although on overcast or wet days they sometimes forage during daylight hours. They rest in the shade of trees, shrubs or rocks, usually near a waterhole, moving out to graze in the late afternoon. They are gregarious and are often seen in groups of 3-8, although larger groups of up to 30 animals gather for safety if they have been disturbed by humans or Dingos. Group membership changes frequently and males groom each other regularly. When alarmed they hiss and thump the ground with their hindfeet as they hop rapidly away. Males are often seen alone, probably searching for female mates, and have been recorded travelling within a home range as large as 76 ha. **Development** Antilopine Wallaroos are thought to breed throughout the year, with a peak of births in the early dry season and towards the end of the wet season. A single young is born some 34 days after mating and attaches firmly to one of the 4 teats in the mother's pouch, vacating the pouch permanently at about 38 weeks, thereafter suckling at foot until about 12 months old.
Diet Grasses. **Habitat** Open savanna woodlands and open monsoonal forests, usually in flat or undulating country. **Traces** Scats are oval, square or round pellets, 15-25 mm across, containing coarse plant fragments. **Status** Secure.
Head-body 775-1200 mm. **Tail** 675-890 mm. **Weight** 16-49 kg. Males are much larger than females.

Onychogalea unguifera

Macropus antilopinus.

Agile Wallaby

Macropus agilis

The Agile Wallaby is the most common macropod found along the coast of tropical Australia. Sandy brown above and light buff to whitish below, it has a whitish stripe along the cheek and thigh, a dark-brown stripe down the forehead, a long black tipped tail and black edged ears. The long pointed face has a partially naked muzzle. Like other macropods the hindfeet lack a first digit, the second and third are fused with a double claw for grooming, while the fourth is much longer than the others. **Behaviour** Active during the late afternoon and night, Agile Wallabies rest in the heat of the day in dense vegetation. They are gregarious animals, living in groups of up to 10 individuals and congregating in much larger mobs when food is short. During the breeding season dominant males monopolise females on heat, staying close to them and keeping other males away. Agile Wallabies are very alert and nervous. When alarmed they thump their hind feet and hop rapidly away with the head held high, the tail horizontal and the forearms extended. **Development** Agile Wallabies have a lifespan of up to 12 years. Females are sexually mature at 12 months, males at about 14 months, and breeding takes place throughout the year. Females mate soon after giving birth, producing a single embryo that remains dormant until the pouch is empty. After a pregnancy of 29-31 days, the newborn attaches firmly to one of 4 teats in the mother's pouch. The infant stays in the pouch for 7-8 months and then suckles at foot until weaned at 10-12 months old. **Diet** Grasses, sedges, leaves, fruits and roots dug up with the forepaws. **Habitat** Along creeks in open forests and adjacent grasslands, and coastal sand dunes. **Traces** Scats are oval, square or round pellets, 15-25 mm across, containing coarse plant fragments. **Status** Secure. **Head-body** 593-850 mm. **Tail** 587-840 mm. **Weight** 9-29 kg. Males are much larger than females.

Red-necked Wallaby

Macropus rufogriseus

This species is known as Bennett's Wallaby in Tasmania and the Bass Strait Islands, where it is darker with a shaggier coat. The fur is soft and deep, dark-brown to reddish-brown above with pale-tan to white tips, and reddish-brown on the neck. The belly and chest are light-grey, the upper lip has a white stripe, the nose, paws and longest toe are black. Females are paler. The tail is well-furred with a brushy tip. The hindfeet have no first digit, the second and third are fused with a double claw, and the fourth is much longer than the others. **Behaviour** Red-necked Wallabies sleep by day in dense vegetation, emerging in the late afternoon (or earlier on cool days) to follow well-defined runways to feeding sites where they often congregate in groups of 30 or more. Males are generally solitary and occupy a home range of about 32 ha. Female home ranges are around 12 ha and overlap close female relatives. In the breeding season males range widely searching for females on heat, and establish dominance hierarchies by fighting and ritualised aggression. Subordinate males are excluded from mating by dominant males and females. Young females settle close to their mother, but males are forced out of their mother's home range at about 2 years of age. **Development** Red-necked Wallabies have a lifespan of up to 18 years. Females are sexually mature at 11-21 months, males at 13-19 months. Mainland animals breed throughout the year, while those in Tasmania breed from January to July. Females mate soon after giving birth, but the embryo remains dormant until the pouch is empty (although in Tasmania the embryo remains dormant until the next breeding season). After a pregnancy of 29-30 days 1-2 young are born and each attaches firmly to one of the 4 teats in the mother's pouch. Young leave the pouch at 40-43 weeks, and for the following month are left in a hiding place while the mother feeds. Thereafter they suckle at foot until 12-17 months old. **Diet** Grasses and herbs. **Habitat** Wet and dry sclerophyll forests and woodlands with grassy areas and a dense understorey; and tall coastal heaths. **Traces** Well-worn runways to feeding areas. Scats are oval to round pellets of grass fragments, 10-20 mm across and up to about 30 mm long, deposited in groups or strings. **Status** Secure. **Head-body** 660-925 mm. **Tail** 620-880 mm. **Weight** 11-27 kg. Males are much larger than females.

Macropus agilis

Macropus rufogriseus

Parma Wallaby

Macropus parma

A cryptic inhabitant of forests with thick shrubby understoreys, the Parma Wallaby was thought to be extinct in Australia until it was rediscovered near Gosford in 1967. It has thick fur, grey-brown to dark-brown above with a dark stripe from the head to the mid-back, and white stripes along the upper lip, throat, chest and belly. Many animals have a white-tipped tail. The hindfeet have no first digit, the second and third are fused with a double claw, the fourth is much longer than the others. **Behaviour** Active mainly at night, Parma Wallabies rest under shrubs in dense vegetation by day and emerge at or just before dusk to feed, travelling along established runways to small grassy areas where they feed alone or sometimes with 1-2 others. They hop close to the ground, almost horizontally, with their forearms tucked into their sides and the tail curved up slightly. Vocalisations include clucking and hissing sounds. **Development** Females are sexually mature at 12 months, males at 20-24 months. The breeding season extends throughout the year with most births from February to June. Parma Wallabies usually mate 45-105 days after giving birth, although the embryo remains dormant until the pouch is empty. After a pregnancy of 33-36 days the newborn attaches firmly to one of 4 teats in the mother's pouch. It makes its first excursions from the pouch at 23-25 weeks and vacates the pouch at about 30 weeks, thereafter suckling at foot until about 10 months old. **Diet** Grasses and herbs. **Habitat** Rainforests and sclerophyll forests with a dense understorey and grassy sites, usually in montane areas. **Traces** Scats are round, oval or oblong pellets, about 10-15 mm across and 10-20 mm long, containing coarse plant fragments. **Status** Vulnerable; threatened by Fox predation and logging. **Head-body** 445-530 mm. **Tail** 405-545 mm. **Weight** 3.2-5.9 kg. Males are larger than females.

Swamp Wallaby

Wallabia bicolor

A common inhabitant of the dense forest understorey, the Swamp Wallaby has coarse fur, dark-brown to black flecked with yellow above, and red-brown to yellow-brown below. The cheeks and shoulders have a light-yellow to red-brown or black stripe; the paws, feet and occasionally the end of the tail are very dark-brown. The hindfeet have no first digit, the second and third are fused with a double claw for grooming, and the fourth is much longer than the others. **Behaviour** Swamp Wallabies are generally active from dusk to dawn, resting in thick undergrowth during the day and moving out to more open grassy areas at night. Essentially solitary, they have home ranges around 2-6 ha or more, and sometimes feed in small groups. Moving slowly they seem relatively uncoordinated with the tail held high, and they often make high leaps in long grass. When moving fast they hold the head low and the tail horizontal. **Development** Sexual mature at 15-18 months, Swamp Wallabies may live to about 15 years. When dingo predation is high they breed year round, but when predation is low they are more seasonal, with most births occurring between April and November. Females mate again about 7 days before giving birth, producing a single embryo that remains dormant until the pouch is empty. After a pregnancy of 33-38 days the newborn attaches firmly to one of the 4 teats in the mother's pouch, which it vacates at about 36 weeks, thereafter suckling at foot until about 15 months old. **Diet** General browse of shrubs, pine seedlings, rushes, fungi, vines, ferns and grasses. **Habitat** Rainforests, sclerophyll forests and woodlands with a dense understorey; and heathlands, to 1200 m. **Traces** Scats are oval to round pellets 20 mm or more across, deposited in groups, or in unsegmented cylinders in spring. They are usually brown when broken, comprising coarse plant fragments. **Status** Secure. **Head-body** 665-850 mm. **Tail** 640-865 mm. **Weight** 10-22 kg. Males are larger than females.

Macropus parma

Wallabia bicolor

Tammar Wallaby

Macropus eugenii

One of the smallest wallabies, the Tammar Wallaby has long, soft fur, dark grey-brown flecked with light-grey above, with reddish-brown patches on the flanks and limbs. It is paler below with a white muzzle, a white stripe on the cheek and a dark stripe down the forehead. The ears are slightly pointed and the nose is naked. The hindfeet have no first digit, the second and third are fused with a double claw, and the fourth is much longer than the others. **Behaviour** Tammar Wallabies are usually active for a few hours after dusk and again for a few hours before dawn. They sleep by day in dense, low vegetation, and move off after dusk, following established run-ways to grassy feeding sites up to 1 km away, and returning before dawn. They are generally solitary with defined overlapping home ranges of some 30 ha, although they sometimes feed with 1-2 others. Males are aggressive during the breeding season when they congregate around females on heat and try to dislodge a successful copulating male. A dominant male will guard a female from other males for up to 8 hours after mating. **Development** Tammar Wallabies have a life expectancy of 13 years or more, although juveniles have a high mortality rate in their first sum-mer. Females become sexually mature while still suckling at about 9 months old, while males mature at about 24 months. Females give birth from January to June and mate 1-2 hours after giving birth, although the embryo typi-cally remains dormant until late December. A single young is born about 40 days later and attaches firmly to one of 4 teats in the mother's pouch. It leaves the pouch permanently at about 36 weeks, and suckles at foot until about 9 months old. **Diet** Native grasses. In droughts they can survive by drinking seawater. **Habitat** Dry sclerophyll forests and woodlands with a dense understorey, mallee thickets, coastal scrubs and heathlands. **Traces** Scats are round, oval or oblong pellets, about 10-15 mm across and 10-25 mm long, containing coarse plant fragments. **Status** Vulnerable; threatened by land clearing and predation by feral Cats. **Head-body** 520-680 mm. **Tail** 330-450 mm. **Weight** 5-10 kg. Males are larger than females.

Western Brush Wallaby

Macropus irma

The Western Brush Wallaby is a grazing kangaroo of the open forests and woodlands of southwestern Australia. It has a pale-grey back sometimes tinged with brown, dis-tinctive black and white ear margins and a white cheek stripe. The long tail has a crest of black hair, and some animals have faint pale bars across the back and tail. The hindfeet have no first digit, the second and third are fused with a double claw for grooming, and the fourth is much longer than the others. **Behaviour** Western Brush Wallabies have not been studied in detail. Unlike most other kangaroos they are most active in the early morning and late afternoon, when they feed in open grassy areas. The remainder of the day is spent resting in the shade or sleeping among low trees or in shrubby thickets. They are gregarious and are often seen in small groups of varying ages. Western Brush Wallabies are well adapted to the open country and are able to move very fast and change direction suddenly, hopping with the head held low and the tail straight out behind. **Development** Females appear to give birth to a single young in April or May. The newborn attaches firmly to one of the 4 teats in the mother's pouch. Young leave the pouch permanently at about 6-7 months old and then suckle at foot. **Diet** Native grasses. They can survive without drinking. **Habitat** Open forests and woodlands with grassy areas and shrubby thickets, mallee and heaths. **Status** Probably secure; vulnerable to predation by Foxes. **Head-body** 830-1530 mm. **Tail** 540-970 mm. **Weight** 7-9 kg.

Macropus eugenii

Macropus irma

Black-striped Wallaby

Macropus dorsalis

Very shy and seldom venturing far from cover, the Black-striped Wallaby shares part of its habitat with the Red-necked Wallaby, with which it is often confused. It can be distinguished by the black stripe running down the centre of its back, from neck to rump and its white thigh stripes. It has sandy to reddish-brown fur, paler on the flanks and grading to almost white below, and white cheek patches. The tail is sparsely-haired and scaly. The hindfeet have no first digit, the second and third are fused with a double claw for grooming, and the fourth is much longer than the others.

Behaviour Active mainly at night, Black-striped Wallabies feed from dusk to dawn in grassy areas with some tree cover, seldom venturing far from cover. They flee if disturbed, moving with a short hopping gait with the back curved, the head low and forearms extended forward and out from the body. During the day they rest in dense vegetation in groups of 20 or more of mixed age and sex, and travel in single file from the resting site along established runways to grazing areas. Adults groom and lick each other frequently and are often seen sparring with each other, probably to establish and maintain dominance hierarchies. Aged males live a solitary existence. **Development** Black-striped Wallabies have a life span of 10-15 years. Females are sexually mature at 14 months, males at 20 months, and they breed year round. Females mate soon after giving birth, although the embryo remains dormant until the pouch is empty. A single young is born after a pregnancy of 33-35 days. The newborn attaches firmly to one of the 4 teats in the mother's pouch, which it vacates at 30 weeks, thereafter suckling at foot until weaned. **Diet** Native grasses. herbs and shrubby vegetation. **Habitat** Closed and open forests and woodlands with a thick understorey, including rainforest margins, brigalow scrub and lantana thickets. **Traces** Scats are oval to round or oblong pellets, often pointed at one end, about 10-15 mm across and 15-20 mm long, containing coarse plant fragments. **Status** Endangered; threatened by land clearing. **Head-body** 530-820 mm. **Tail** 540-830 mm. **Weight** 6-20 kg. Males are much larger than females.

Whiptail Wallaby

Macropus parryi

A slim, graceful kangaroo of the open forests, the Whiptail Wallaby is known for its long, slender tail. It has a triangular face with large brown and white ears, a dark-brown forehead and a contrasting white cheek stripe. It is white below with a light-brown stripe along the neck and shoulder, a white stripe on the hip, dark paws and a dark tip to the tail. The winter coat is light grey above and the summer coat brownish-grey. The hindfeet have no first digit, the second and third are fused with a double claw for grooming, and the fourth is much longer than the others. **Behaviour** Whiptail Wallabies feed mainly around dawn and early morning, resting in the shade until late afternoon and feeding into the night. They are very gregarious and live in mobs of 30-50 animals with a large stable home range of up to 100 ha or more, abutting those of neighbouring mobs. Individuals or small groups have overlapping home ranges within this area and dominance hierarchies are established by aggression and rituals such as grass-pulling with the forepaws. A female on heat is followed by a group of males, but the dominant male keeps the subordinates at a distance. When alarmed they scatter erratically, thumping the ground with the hindfeet as they hop away taking a zig-zag course with the back and tail almost horizontal. Vocalisations include a soft submissive cough, soft clucking during courtship and a threatening growling hiss. **Development** Females are sexually active at 18-24 months, males at 2-3 years. Births occur throughout the year with a peak from March to July. Females mate near the end of the young's pouch life, although the embryo remains dormant until the pouch is empty. After a pregnancy of 34-38 days the single young attaches firmly to one of 4 teats in the mother's pouch. It detaches from the teat at about 23 weeks, vacates the pouch at about 38 weeks and suckles at foot until about 15 months old. **Diet** Grass, herbs and ferns. It seldom needs to drink. **Habitat** Open forest with a grassy understorey, often in hilly areas. **Traces** Scats are deposited in groups or clumped in strings. They are round to oval or square pellets, about 10-20 mm across and 20-40 mm long, containing coarse plant fragments. **Status** Probably secure. **Head-body** 675-955 mm. **Tail** 725-1045 mm. **Weight** 7-26 kg. Males are much larger than females.

Macropus dorsalis

Macropus parryi

Common Wallaroo. Euro

Macropus robustus

The two major subspecies of this large kangaroo differ markedly in their colouration and habitat. The Eastern subspecies is a dark-grey forest-dweller known as the Common Wallaroo. It has fairly coarse, shaggy fur, and some females are bluish-grey, while some males have a reddish band across the shoulders and neck. In central and western Australia it has shorter reddish-brown fur, lives in hot, arid areas, and is known as the Euro. All have a black, naked nose, a short, thick tail and relatively short limbs. **Behaviour** Common Wallaroos shelter from the heat of the day among dense trees, in caves, or under rock ledges, often above their feeding grounds, and emerge in the late afternoon to graze. They are usually solitary and occupy small overlapping home ranges, usually including parts of the lower slopes and nearby plains. Males attain twice the weight of females and establish dominance hierarchies, giving mating preferences to the strongest. During courtship males mark low vegetation with secretions from a chest gland and fight over females on heat, engaging in ritualised boxing matches. When alarmed they make threatening hisses, clucking calls and thump the ground with their hindfeet. Like other wallaroos they stand with their wrists raised, shoulders thrown back and elbows close to their sides. **Development** Sexually mature at 18-24 months, Common Wallaroos may live to 15 years. They breed throughout the year and mate soon after giving birth, although the embryo remains dormant until the pouch is empty. After a pregnancy of about 34 days the newborn attaches firmly to one of 4 teats in the mother's pouch. It leaves the pouch at about 34-37 weeks and suckles at foot until about 14 months old. **Diet** Native grasses and some shrubs. They can survive without drinking. **Habitat** Rocky slopes, stony hills and escarpments, from wet sclerophyll forests to arid tussock grasslands, from the tropics to the subalps. **Traces** Water digs in dry river beds in desert areas. Scats are round, oval or square pellets, about 10-20 mm across and 20-40 mm long, containing fairly coarse plant fragments, and sometimes deposited in clumps. **Status** Probably secure, but rare and vulnerable in Vic. **Head-body** 570-1100 mm. **Tail** 530-900 mm. **Weight** Males to 46.5 kg, females to 25 kg.

Eastern Grey Kangaroo

Macropus giganteus

The Eastern Grey Kangaroo is a large, robust marsupial with soft, deep fur varying from light silver-grey to dark-grey flecked with light-grey above, and usually paler below. Females have a white chest. The forehead is grey, while the paws, feet and tail tip are dark grey to black. It has a hairy nose and no first digits on the hindfeet; the second and third toes are fused with a double claw for grooming, and the fourth is much longer than the others. **Behaviour** Predominantly nocturnal, Eastern Grey Kangaroos rest in the shade and feed from late afternoon to early morning, often in mobs of 10 or more, occupying overlapping home ranges of up to 5 sq km. Males establish dominance hierarchies by fighting and ritualised acts including grass-pulling with the forefeet, and range widely searching for females on heat. Females usually congregate with female relatives and will only mate with dominant males. Old males are usually solitary. Clucking sounds are made between mother and young and during courtship. When alarmed they make guttural coughs and thump their hindfeet as they hop away with the body erect and the tail curved up. They can also swim to avoid predators. **Development** Sexual maturity is reached at about 20-36 months, and they may live for 10-12 years. Breeding occurs year-round with a peak of births in summer or when conditions improve after droughts. Females mate about 11 days after the pouch is vacated, or in good seasons when the pouch young is more than 4 months old (the embryo remains dormant until the pouch is empty). After a pregnancy of 33-38 days the newborn attaches firmly to one of 4 teats in the mother's pouch, which it vacates at about 11 months, suckling at foot until 18 months old. Twins have been recorded. **Diet** Grass and low shrubby vegetation. **Habitat** Dry sclerophyll forests, woodlands and low open scrub, with grassy areas, from sea level to more than 1000 m. **Traces** Water digs in dry desert watercourses. Scats are oval to squarish pellets, about 10-20 mm across and 20-30 mm long, containing fine-textured green to brown plant fragments, and sometimes deposited in large clumps. **Status** Secure. **Head-body** 500-1212 mm. **Tail** 430-1100 mm. **Weight** Males to 75 kg, females to 40 kg.

Macropus robustus

Macropus giganteus

Western Grey Kangaroo

Macropus fuliginosus

Similar in many respects to the Eastern Grey Kangaroo, this species has light to dark chocolate-brown fur, often flecked with grey above, and paler below. It has dark-brown to black paws, feet and tail tip, and buff patches on the legs and forearms. It has a finely haired muzzle and large ears fringed with white hairs. The hindfeet have no first digit, the second and third are fused with a double claw for groom-ing, and the fourth is much longer than the others. **Behaviour** Western Grey Kangaroos rest by day in the shelter of trees and shrubs, and feed from late afternoon to early morning. Mobs of 40-50 range within a discrete territory, with subgroups of 2-4 animals occupying overlapping home ranges of up to 8 sq km. Males have a strong, distinctive odour and establish dominance hierar-chies by fighting and ritualised acts such as tree-gouging with the front claws. They range widely searching for females on heat. Females usually congregate with female relatives, form their own dominance hierarchies and will only mate with dominant males. Old males are usually solitary. When alarmed they make guttural coughs and thump their hindfeet, hopping away with the body erect and the tail curved up. **Development** Females are sexually mature at about 16 months, males at 20 months. They breed year round with a peak of births from September to March. Females mate 2-10 days after the pouch is vacated. After a pregnancy of 30.5 days the single newborn (rarely twins) attaches firmly to one of 4 teats in the mother's pouch, which it vacates at about 42 weeks, suckling at foot until about 17 months old. **Diet** Native grasses, herbs and shrubs. **Habitat** Dry open forests, woodlands, open scrubs, wet and dry heaths. **Traces** Similar to the Eastern Grey Kangaroo. **Status** Secure. **Head-body** 520-1225 mm. **Tail** 425-1000 mm. **Weight** Males to 66 kg, females to 29 kg.

Red Kangaroo

Macropus rufus

The Red Kangaroo is one of the largest living marsupials, and males are very powerfully built. The fur is reddish-brown above and paler below, although eastern females are blue-grey. A broad white stripe runs along the cheek, while the muzzle has black and white markings with a partially naked tip. The hindfeet have no first digit, the second and third are fused with a double claw for grooming, and the fourth is much longer than the others. **Behaviour** Red Kangaroos rest during the heat of the day in dusty scrapes under bushes or shrubs, and feed from late afternoon to early morning, although on cool, wet days they may be active throughout the day. They live alone or in groups of 2-10, occupying a home range of around 8 sq km. This area increases in droughts when mobs of several hundred may gather to feed and drink. Males congregate around females on heat and establish dominance hierarchies by boxing. The largest males have exclusive mating rights. Young males range widely and old males are solitary. When alarmed they make a loud cough and thump their hindfeet, hopping rapidly away with the body and tail horizontal. **Development** Sexual maturity is reached at 2-3 years, although in good years females can mate 6 months earlier and continue to breed throughout the year. Mating takes place soon after birth, although the embryo remains dormant until the pouch is empty. Pregnancy lasts 33 days and the newborn attaches firmly to one of 4 teats in the mother's pouch. It leaves the pouch at around 8 months and suckles at foot for another 3-4 months. In prolonged droughts more than half the pouch young die and females stop mating. They may live 20 years. **Diet** Native grasses, herbs and shrubs. They can survive without water if the food is green. **Habitat** Dry woodlands, scrub, grasslands, plains and deserts. **Traces** Similar to the Eastern Grey Kangaroo. **Status** Secure. **Head-body** 740-1400 mm. **Tail** 640-1000 mm. **Weight** Males to 95 kg, females to 37 kg.

Macropus fuliginosus

Macropus rufus

Grey-headed Flying-fox

Pteropus poliocephalus

The largest Australian bat with a wingspan of up to 1.3 m, the Grey-headed Flying-fox has long fur, dark-brown above and grey below, often flecked with white or yellow-brown. It is tailless and has a light-grey, Fox-like head with a reddish-brown mantle encircling the neck. Thick leg fur extends to the ankle. The eyes are large and the ears simple. Both first and second fingers of the forelimbs are clawed and used for climbing. **Behaviour** Grey-headed Flying-foxes navigate by sight and avoid flying in complete darkness. They leave their daytime roost at dusk and fly to foraging areas up to 50 km away, travelling at 35 kph or more, and returning before dawn. They congregate in large camps, usually in gullies near water, with good tree cover, hanging from the branches wrapped in their wings. Pregnant females form maternity camps about 2 weeks before giving birth from September to October, and are joined by adult males as the young are being weaned from February to March. Camps comprise a few hundred to hundreds of thousands of bats, depending on the availability of food resources. Juveniles and old males keep guard on the edge of the camp while breeding adult males mark territories and attract females by smearing secretions from their shoulder glands on their neck fur and branches. Males defend a small area by fighting, wing-slapping and shrieking. Adults usually disperse in winter, travelling up to 750 km, alone or in small groups. Juveniles and a few adults form winter camps near reliable food sources. **Development** Sexually maturity is reached at 18 months, although males first breed at about 30 months, and are only fertile in March and April. A single young is born in September or October, about 6 months after mating, and suckles from a teat in the mother's armpit, clinging to her belly fur and carried when she forages for 3-4 weeks, until well-furred. Young are then left in the camp at night while the mother forages, and are suckled on her return. They can fly at 3-4 months and are weaned at 5-6 months. **Diet** Pollen and nectar, from more than 80 plant species, mainly eucalypts and wattles, supplemented fruits, mainly figs, and leaves. They can drink seawater. **Habitat** Wet and dry sclerophyll forests, rainforests, paperbark swamps and mangroves, to 700 m. **Traces** Fibrous remnants of chewed fruit and flower clusters beneath trees. Scats are pungent, shapeless masses, beneath roosting and feeding trees. **Status** Secure. **Head-body** 230-290 mm. **Forearm** 138-180 mm. **Weight** 600-1050 g.

Little Red Flying-fox

Pteropus scapulatus

The Little Red Flying-fox is the smallest of the Australian flying-foxes, with a wingspan of about 1 m. This winged placental mammal has soft, short, dense fur, reddish-brown to yellowish-brown above and paler below with a light-brown to yellow collar encircling the neck, patches of creamy-brown where the wings meet the shoulders, pale yellow hairs on the underside of the translucent wing membranes, and sparsely furred or naked legs. The Fox-like head has large eyes and simple ears. It has no tail, and the first 2 fingers of the forelimbs have claws. **Behaviour** Active at night and on overcast afternoons, Little Red Flying-foxes are highly nomadic and travel long distances, navigating by sight. They are not very manoeuvrable and often crash-land into trees. In October-November they congregate in camps of up to one million (depending on available food sources) with hundreds sharing the same tree, hanging by their feet, wrapped in their wings. Columns of bats leave at dusk, spiralling around before heading to feeding sites. Juveniles live on the periphery of the camps while adult males gather harems of 2-5 females in small territories, marked by secretions of their shoulder glands, and defended from other males. After mating, around February, they tend to move to new camps in small, single sex groups, or join the camps of other Flying-foxes. **Development** Sexually mature at 18 months, they mate from October to January. A single young is born in April-May and suckles from a teat in the mother's armpit. Young cling to their mother until well-furred at about one month. They are then left at the roost while she forages. They can fly at 2 months and are cared for until they are several months old and have learned to forage and navigate. **Diet** Nectar and pollen of eucalypt and melaleuca trees, soft fruit, sap and sugary insect secretions licked from leaves. **Habitat** Rainforests, mangroves, sclerophyll forests, paperbark swamps and woodlands. **Traces** Similar to the Grey-headed Flying-fox. **Status** Secure. **Head-body** 190-240 mm. **Forearm** 120-155 mm. **Weight** 310-605 g.

Pteropus poliocephalus

Pteropus scapulatus

Black Flying-fox

Pteropus alecto

The Black Flying-fox is a large coastal bat with short, soft, black fur, often flecked with grey below and sometimes reddish-brown on the shoulders and back of the neck. It is tailless with a Fox-like head with large eyes and simple ears. The toes and first and second fingers have long, curved claws. **Behaviour** Black Flying-foxes roost by day in the branches of large trees, hanging upside down wrapped in their wings. In September and October they congregate in camps of several hundred to hundreds of thousands of bats, often shared with Grey-headed and Little Red Flying-foxes. They leave for nocturnal feeding grounds at dusk and fly with rapid wing beats at 35-40 kph, travelling up to 50 km and navigating by sight. Old males usually live on the camp periphery and guard the camp from intruders. In the breeding season large males establish territories about 1 m across along branches marked by secretions from their shoulder glands. Their testes descend into a prominent position and they spend much time grooming and displaying their genitalia to attract females. At the end of the breeding season most bats disperse to live alone or in small groups. **Development** Mating takes place in March and April and a single young is born from August to November (about 3 months later in the north) and suckles from a teat in the mother's armpit. It is carried for 3-4 weeks until well-furred, clinging to its mother's fur with its feet, it is then left in the camp at night. It can fly at 2 months and is independent at about 13 weeks. **Diet** Mainly blossoms of eucalypts and paperbarks, soft fruit, sap, and some leaves. They can drink seawater. **Habitat** Rainforests, mangroves, wet sclerophyll forests and woodlands. **Traces** Similar to the Grey-headed Flying-fox. **Status** Secure. **Head-body** 186-300 mm. **Forearm** 138-191 mm. **Weight** 500-880 g.

Spectacled Flying-fox

Pteropus conspicillatus

An essential pollinator and distributor of rainforest seeds, the Spectacled Flying-fox is named for the patches of pale-yellow fur around the eyes and along the muzzle. It has a prominent yellow or silver-blond collar partially encircling the neck and soft black body fur often flecked with white. It is tailless with a Fox-like head with large eyes and simple ears. The 5 toes and first and second fingers bear long, curved claws. **Behaviour** Spectacled Flying-foxes roost by day hanging from the branches of large trees, wrapped in their wings. They navigate by sight and fly off at dusk to feed in flowering and fruiting trees. Well-defined territories are established in feed trees, and intruders are chased away with much shrieking and wing-slapping, although they usually leave with a fruit. They form more or less permanent camps, some comprising many thousands of bats, in coastal sites in or close to the rainforest. During the mating season males attract females and mark territories by smearing their neck fur and branches with a red fluid containing secretions from sebaceous glands on the neck, mixed with a strong-smelling liquid secreted from the erect penis. Pregnant females leave the coastal camps and form maternity camps in highland regions. **Development** Sexually mature at 2 years, they mate from April to May and give birth to a single young from October to December. Newborn suckle from a teat in the mother's armpit and are carried for 1-2 weeks until well-furred. They are then left in the camp at night, are weaned at about 12 weeks and become independent at 5 months. **Diet** Blossom and fruits. They drink seawater while skimming over the surface. **Habitat** Rainforests, mangroves, paperbark swamps and wet sclerophyll forests. **Traces** Similar to the Grey-headed Flying-fox. **Status** Vulnerable; threatened by land clearing and orchardists. **Head-body** 220-240 mm. **Forearm** 155-181 mm. **Weight** 500-850 g.

Pteropus alecto

Pteropus conspicillatus

Common Blossom-bat
Syconycteris australis

Also known as the Queensland Blossom-bat, this mouse-sized species is an important
pollinator in the tropics, feeding on nectar obtained with its long, thin, brush-tipped
tongue and slim, pointed muzzle. It has long, soft, reddish-brown to fawn fur
extending to the ankle, and is tailless with a Fox-like head, simple rounded ears
and obvious upper incisor teeth which are weak and slender. It has a large claw on
the first finger and a tiny claw on the second finger. **Behaviour** Common Blossom-
bats roost by day alone or in small groups in dense foliage, hanging upside down with the wings
wrapped around the body. They navigate by sight, flying 3-5 m above the ground, often following tracks
through the forest to feeding sites up to 4 km away. They hover over selected blossoms and crash-land to feed, gathering nectar with the tongue. Pollen lodges on scale-like projections on the fur and is collected by grooming after a
bout of feeding. Individuals defend food sources from intruders, chasing them away, shrieking and clapping their
wingtips together. They change roosts frequently within a 50 m radius and move to the warmer edge of the rainforest
in winter, becoming torpid for up to 12 hours on cold days or when food is scarce. **Development** Females give birth
to a single young in October-November and another between February and April, although in tropical areas they
may breed throughout the year. The young suckles from a teat in the mother's armpit for up to 3 months and is carried with her until well-furred. **Diet** Nectar and pollen, supplemented by some fruit and leaf in the tropics.
Habitat Rainforests, wet sclerophyll forests, paperbark swamps and heathlands. **Status** Probably secure.
Head-body 40-71 mm. **Forearm** 38-45 mm. **Weight** 13-26 g.

Eastern Tube-nosed Bat
Nyctimene robinsoni

Also known as the Queensland Tube-nosed Bat, this distinctive bat is characterised by
its prominent tubular nostrils which extend 5-6 mm beyond the muzzle, and by the
pale yellow-green spots on its wings and ears. The fur is long and soft, grey-brown
to light-brown above and paler below, usually with a dark-brown stripe along the
centre of the back. It has simple rounded ears, a short, free tail and claws on both
first and second fingers. **Behaviour** Eastern Tube-nosed Bats roost by day alone or
sometimes in groups of 4-5 in trees close to their feeding sites, hanging from a branch wrapped
in their wings, and closely resembling a dead leaf. Some bats remain in the same area for 3 years or more,
while others are nomadic and may change roosts daily to take advantage of fruiting trees. Large feeding groups
sometimes form around trees and individuals will aggressively defend a feeding territory. They have good vision and
avoid flying in total darkness. They forage in the forest understorey, flying close to the ground along forest tracks,
hovering with ease, often making bleating calls. **Development** Little is known about their development. They give
birth to a single young between October and December which suckles from a teat in the mother's armpit and is carried with her until well-furred. **Diet** Fruits, particularly figs, Blue Quandongs and Burdekin Plums, and banksia
blossoms. They can survive without drinking. **Habitat** Rainforests, wet and dry sclerophyll forests, woodlands and
heathlands. **Status** Probably secure. **Head-body** 80-93 mm. **Tail** 20-25 mm. **Forearm** 60-70 mm. **Weight** 30-56 g.

Syconycteris australis

Nyctimene robinsoni

Ghost Bat

Macroderma gigas

Also known as the False Vampire Bat, this large predatory bat has a wingspan of about 500 mm, long soft fur, fawn-grey to dove-grey above and pale-grey to white below. The ears are very large, joined above the head and sparsely-haired with a forked lobe partially covering the aperture. They have no tail. The eyes are large and a large, simple noseleaf projects above the snout. **Behaviour** Active mainly at night, Ghost Bats roost by day in deep caves, rock fissures and mines, hanging from the ceiling at least 25 cm apart and 2 m above the floor, congregating in colonies of up to 1500 in the breeding season. Mothers wean their young on prey brought back to the roost, and take juveniles with them to hunt. They fly fast and direct with the head held high, orienting by sight and by the intermittent use of echo-location, emitting signals through the mouth, foraging in preferred sites about 2 km from their roost. They often locate prey by sight and sound while sitting on a branch, and swoop on small terrestrial animals, enveloping them in their wings and biting them to death. Other bats are sometimes caught in flight. Prey is consumed at an established feeding site, usually in a small cave or rock overhang. They make twittering and cricket-like calls. **Development** Mating takes place in May, and a single young is born in July and August. The newborn weighs 20 g and suckles from a teat in the mother's armpit for several months. It is carried until well-furred at 4 weeks, and then left in the roost until able to fly by 7 weeks. **Diet** A variety of animals including insects, birds, lizards, frogs, mice and bats. **Habitat** Rainforests, wet and dry sclerophyll forests and arid woodlands. **Traces** Accumulations of bones and other animal remains at feeding sites. **Status** Vulnerable; threatened by mining of roosting caves. **Head-body** 98-130 mm. **Forearm** 96-113 mm. **Weight** 74-165 g.

Northern Blossom-bat

Macroglossus minimus

An important pollinator of paperbark trees, the Northern Blossom-bat probes flowers for nectar and pollen with its long, narrow, brush-tipped tongue. It is very similar to the Common Blossom-bat with long, soft fur, fawn to reddish-brown above and paler on the chest, but can be distinguished by the presence of flap-like membranes ("pyjamas") on each leg. It has a small, rudimentary tail and a Fox-like head with a tapering muzzle and simple, broad, rounded ears. The first finger has a large claw and the second finger a tiny claw. The incisor teeth are slender, weak, and often malformed. **Behaviour** Northern Blossom-bats roost by day alone or in small groups in thick foliage, under loose bark, in tree hollows, rolled banana leaves and buildings, hanging upside down wrapped in their wings. They have an acute sense of smell and navigate by sight, leaving the roost at dusk, flying slowly and foraging at night in forests and woodlands for flowering and fruiting trees. They hover beside or land on a flower and lap up the nectar with their long, bristly tongue. Pollen sticks to the fur and is licked off during a grooming session. Individuals chase other bats away from their feeding trees, screeching and slapping their wings. Adult males have a pink, V-shaped gland on the chest, producing a pungent smell which probably attracts females. **Development** Copulation may occur at any time of year, and births have been recorded from February to March and August to October. The single young suckles from a teat under the mother's armpit, clinging constantly to her fur with its clawed feet for 6-10 days. It then remains at the roost while she forages, and can fly by 40 days. Males become sexually mature at 7 months. **Diet** Nectar, pollen and some fruits, particularly figs. **Habitat** Rainforests, mangroves, paperbark woodlands, bamboo thickets, banana plantations and monsoon scrub. **Status** Probably secure. **Head-body** 49-67 mm. **Forearm** 37-43 mm. **Weight** 10-20 g.

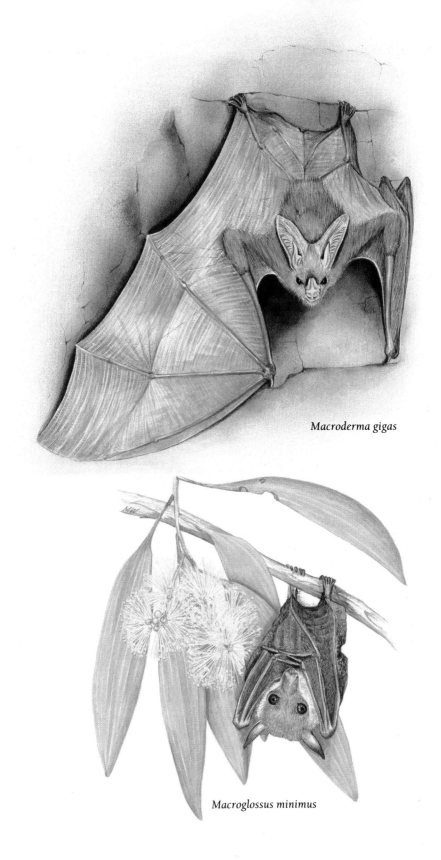

Macroderma gigas

Macroglossus minimus

Orange Leaf-nosed Bat   *Rhinonycteris aurantius*

The Orange Leaf-nosed Bat is a small, insectivorous bat with fine golden fur, sometimes darker-tipped, with dark bands across the eyes. There are colonies of brown,
yellow and all white bats. It has small eyes, sharply pointed ears and a complex
noseleaf above the snout with a horseshoe-shaped indented lower part, a scalloped upper section with deep pits and a forward projection in the centre. The
tail protrudes slightly beyond the tail membrane. **Behaviour** Active mainly at
night, Orange Leaf-nosed Bats roost by day in the dry season in deep, very warm and humid
caves in limestone formations, usually with difficult access to deter predators such as the Ghost Bat.
They roost in colonies ranging from 5 to 20,000 or more individuals, and disperse during the wet season, from
November to February, probably to live in the forest. Despite their inability to maintain a high body temperature
they do not cluster together, but space themselves 10-15 cm apart, suspended from the roof with the head hanging
down or clinging to a wall with the forearms spread well apart, with their wings folded against the sides of the body.
At dusk they leave the roost to hunt for insects in nearby forests and woodlands, returning frequently to groom and
digest their prey. They fly with fast wing beats, zig-zag close to the ground searching for insects, and are often seen
following roads at night. They have good sight, but also use echo-location to detect flying insects up to 2 m away,
emitting ultrasonic signals through the nose and directing them with the noseleaf. **Development** Females are sexually mature at 7 months, males at 18 months. They mate in July and females give birth to a single young in late
December or early January. The young suckles from a teat in the mother's armpit, grows quickly and is weaned in
late February. **Diet** Moths, beetles and flying termites, with some wasps, ants and other insects caught on the wing
or gleaned from the foliage. **Habitat** Mangroves, spinifex grasslands, vine thickets, dense palm forests and woodlands. **Status** Vulnerable; threatened by human disturbance of roosts. **Head-body** 44-56 mm. **Tail** 23-29 mm.
Forearm 45-51 mm. **Weight** 6-12 g.

Dusky Leaf-nosed Bat   *Hipposideros ater*

The Dusky Lea-fnosed Bat is a small, delicate, insectivorous bat with long, soft fur,
light-grey above with blackish-brown to orange tips, and slightly paler below. It has
small eyes, very large, broad and slightly pointed ears and a simple noseleaf with
a horseshoe-shaped lower ridge above the snout. The tail protrudes slightly
beyond the tail membrane. **Behaviour** Active mainly at night, Dusky Leaf-nosed
Bats roost by day in caves, crevices, mines and sometimes tree-hollows, preferring
small, hot, humid caves. They hang by their toes from the ceiling, 10-15 cm apart, wings against
their sides and head hanging down. They roost alone or in colonies of 10-30 bats, although 300 have been
recorded. In the Northern Territory they are preyed upon by Ghost Bats which often inhabit their roost sites. They
leave the roost at dusk and hunt for insects in dense vegetation, flying low to the ground, slow and flutteringly, often
changing direction and hovering. They sometimes forage in small groups and return frequently to the cave entrance
to digest their prey. They have good sight, but use echo-location to detect flying insects and navigate in darkness,
emitting ultrasonic signals through the nose and directing them with the noseleaf. **Development** Dusky Leaf-nosed
Bats mate from April to May and give birth to a single young from October to December. Newborn cling to one of 2
false teats in the mother's pubic region while she forages for the first 2 weeks, and suckle from a teat under each
armpit. They then often cling to her shoulders and practice wing-flapping and echo-locating. They reach adult size
after 6-8 weeks and accompany their mother on foraging expeditions. **Diet** Moths, mosquitoes and other flying
insects caught on the wing. **Habitat** Rainforests, open forests, dry vine thickets, savannah woodlands and spinifex
grasslands. **Status** Probably secure, but very sparse. **Head-body** 33-50 mm. **Tail** 22-28 mm. **Forearm** 34-41 mm.
Weight 3-6 g.

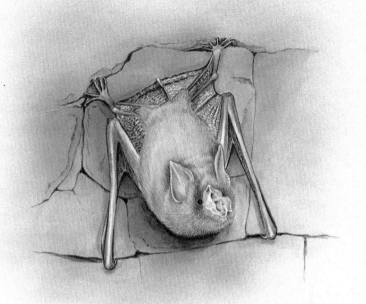

Rhinonycteris aurantius

Hipposideros ater

Eastern Horseshoe Bat

Rhinolophus megaphyllus

The Eastern Horseshoe Bat is a small, insectivorous bat with long, soft, greyish-brown fur, although some northern animals are orange-brown. It has large, simple and sharply-pointed ears, very small eyes and a complex noseleaf above the snout with a horseshoe-shaped lower part, a scalloped upper section and a fleshy central projection. The tail does not protrude beyond the tail membrane.
Behaviour Active mainly at night, Eastern Horseshoe Bats have good eyesight but use echo-location to navigate and locate prey in the dark, emitting high-pitched sounds through the nose and directing them with the noseleaf. They travel up to 2 km from their roost sites, foraging for flying insects among dense vegetation close to the ground and in the tree canopy, flying slowly, changing direction suddenly and hovering. They can take spiders from the ground and also hang in shrubs 1-2 m high, darting out to catch prey. Insects are often eaten at a hunting perch. They roost by day in warm, humid sites in caves, mines and buildings, hanging from the roof 15-20 cm apart with their feet together and head hanging down. Colonies typically comprise about 20 bats, but females congregate in maternity colonies of 15-2000 bats in spring, choosing warm, humid caves to rear their young. In the tropics they may form large, non-breeding colonies of up to 2000 bats in the dry season. In temperate areas they disperse in winter and roost alone in cooler parts of the caves, becoming torpid during the day or hibernating from April to June. **Development** Males become sexually mature early in their second year, females in their second or third year. They mate in June and a single young is born in November. Newborn suckle from a teat under the mother's armpit and are carried in flight, clinging to a false pubic teat, legs wrapped around her chest, until well-furred at 4-5 weeks. They are then left clustered in the maternity cave while she forages, and are weaned at 8 weeks. **Diet** Moths, beetles, cockroaches, flies, wasps, other flying insects and spiders. **Habitat** Rain-forests, open coastal scrub and tall forests. **Traces** Insect remains beneath hunting perches. Scats are small, friable, about 5 mm long, composed of insect fragments, and deposited at roosting sites. **Status** Secure, but vulnerable in Vic. where there are only 3 maternity caves. **Head-body** 40-60 mm. **Forearm** 44-52 mm. **Tail** 35-45 mm. **Weight** 7-14 g.

Common Sheathtail Bat

Taphozous georgianus

A widespread insectivorous bat, the Common Sheathtail Bat has dark-brown fur above with a creamy-white base. It is light-brown below with flecks of grey under the arms and sparse yellow hairs under the base of the tail. The tail protrudes through the tail-membrane and slides freely giving the hindlimbs more freedom of movement, allowing the bat to move quadrupedally. The face is Dog-like with large ridged ears and a prominent lobe partially covering the ear aperture.
Behaviour Active at night, Common Sheathtail Bats roost alone or with up to 260 others in caves, rock fissures and mine shafts. They roost in the twilight zone near the cave entrance, well-spaced, clinging to the walls fairly high above the ground. If disturbed they scuttle away, crab-like, and hide in a crevice. Individuals use many different caves, relocating regularly, and females may form maternity colonies. They have good vision and can detect insects up to 10 m away in complete darkness, using echo-location, emitting high-pitched sounds through the mouth. They emerge at dusk and fly high and fast, often hunting in a grid pattern, catching and eating insects in flight. Fat reserves are built up in summer and used in winter. On cold days they cluster together and become torpid to save energy. **Development** Males produce sperm in summer and autumn and store it until mating from late August to September. A single young is born in November-December. The newborn is well-developed, fully-furred with open eyes, and suckles from a teat in the mother's armpit. It is carried while the mother forages until able to fly at 3-4 weeks. Adult size is reached in 3-4 months. Females first mate at 9 months, males at 21 months. Only about 10 per cent of females and 3 per cent of males live more than 4 years. **Diet** Flying insects, particularly beetles. **Habitat** Wet and dry sclerophyll forests, paperbark forests, vine forests, monsoon forests, woodlands, spinifex and grasslands. **Status** Secure. **Head-body** 61-89 mm. **Tail** 20-40 mm. **Forearm** 61-75 mm. **Weight** 16-51 g. (depending on accumulated body fat).

Rhinolophus megaphyllus

Taphozous georgianus

Hill's Sheathtail Bat

Taphozous hilli

Often found roosting with the Common Sheathtail Bat, this small insectivorous bat was
thought to be the same species until recently. It is, however, a slightly different
colour and the males have a small, pouched neck gland. The fur is rich clove-
brown above and grades to light-brown on the rump. The belly fur is light-buff,
tipped with olive-brown, and the wings are greyish-brown. The tail protrudes
through the tail-membrane and slides freely giving the hindlimbs more movement,
allowing the bat to move quadrupedally. The face is Dog-like with large ridged ears with a
prominent lobe partially covering the ear aperture. **Behaviour** Active at night, Hill's Sheathtail Bats
roost in small colonies of up to 25 individuals in caves, rock fissures and mine shafts. They prefer to live near the
cave entrance in the twilight zone, clinging to the walls with their clawed toes. When disturbed they scuttle around
the walls like small crabs and hide in crevices. Pregnant females are reluctant to fly and roost in tiny crevices. They
emerge from their roosts at dusk and hunt for insects above and around trees. They have good vision and can detect
insects at night using echo-location, emitting high-pitched sounds through the mouth. The pouch surrounding the
male's neck gland enlarges in summer, and probably plays a role in mating behaviour. **Development** Males appear
to be fertile all year. Females give birth to a single young between spring and late autumn. Newborn are large and
well-furred, and suckle from a teat in the mother's armpit. **Diet** Insects. **Habitat** Arid and semi-arid woodlands,
spinifex grasslands and acacia shrublands in rocky, hilly country. **Status** Probably secure. **Head-body** 63-81 mm.
Tail 23-38 mm. **Forearm** 60-72 mm. **Weight** 20-29 g.

Yellow-bellied Sheathtail Bat

Saccolaimus flaviventris

The Yellow-bellied Sheathtail Bat is the largest Australian sheathtail-bat. It has glossy
black fur above and contrasting white or creamy-yellow belly fur. Both sexes have a
pouched neck gland which is well-developed in males and reduced to a rudimentary fold of skin in females. The wings are long and narrow and the tips fold back
over the membrane at rest. The tip of the tail is covered with bristles and appears
to protrude through the tail-membrane, although it is connected. The tail slides
freely, making it easier for the bat to use its hindlimbs. The head is Dog-like, mostly naked, with
black skin and thick, leathery, ribbed ears with a prominent lobe partially covering the ear aperture. Only
the thumbs of the forelimbs have a claw. **Behaviour** Active at night, Yellow-bellied Sheathtail Bats are good
climbers and fly fast and direct with slow wing beats, hunting high above the forest canopy and in forest clearings,
often chasing each other in flight. They have good vision and are able to navigate and detect flying insects at night by
echo-location, emitting audible calls through the mouth while flying. They roost alone or in groups of up to 10 bats in
buildings and large tree hollows, occasionally using the abandoned nests of Sugar Gliders. Secretions from the neck
gland may be used by males to mark territories. In southern areas they migrate to warmer locations in winter.
Development Births have been recorded from early December to mid-March, and males appear to be able to reproduce at any time of year. **Diet** Flying insects, particularly beetles, grasshoppers and moths. **Habitat** Most habitats
from rainforests, sclerophyll forests and woodlands to grasslands and deserts. **Status** Vulnerable; threatened by the
logging of old trees. **Head-body** 70-92 mm. **Forearm** 65-82 mm. **Tail** 20-35 mm. **Weight** 30-60 g.

Taphozous hilli

Saccolaimus flaviventris

White-striped Freetail Bat
Nyctinomus australis

Although fierce-looking, the White-striped Freetail Bat is quite docile. The fur is short and dense, chocolate-brown to reddish-brown or black above, paler below with a distinct white stripe along the junction of the wings and body, and occasionally with white patches on the chest. It has fleshy, rounded, strongly-ribbed ears, almost touching above the head, and a deeply-wrinkled upper lip. Both sexes have a deep, wide throat pouch of unknown function. The toes are thick, fleshy and fringed with long, stiff, curved hairs. The tail projects well beyond the tail-membrane and the wings are very compact when folded, allowing free movement of the limbs and agile movements on the ground. **Behaviour** Active at night, White-striped Freetail Bats are fast, direct fliers with poor manoeuvrability, and tend to hunt in open areas and high above the canopy. They have difficulty taking off from the ground, and usually crawl onto a rock or tree to launch themselves. They have good sight, and detect insects at night by echo-location, emitting regular, high-pitched, metallic, ting ... ting ... ting calls. They also forage on the ground, scurrying around searching for terrestrial insects. They roost alone or in small colonies of up to 20 bats in tree hollows, under bark and in buildings, sometimes sharing roosts with other bats. Southern populations are thought to migrate to warmer climates in winter. **Development** Females are sexually mature in their first year, and most females reproduce every year. Mating occurs in August and a single young is born in December or January. The infant suckles from a teat in the mother's armpit, and is weaned by March or early May. **Diet** Insects, predominantly moths, with ants and beetles taken from the ground. **Habitat** Sclerophyll forests, woodlands, scrub and urban areas, to at least 1400 m. **Status** Secure, but sparsely distributed in the central desert. **Head-body** 80-100 mm. **Forearm** 55-65 mm. **Tail** 40-60 mm. **Weight** 25-44 g.

Little Freetail Bat
Mormopterus planiceps

A small insectivorous bat with an upturned, hound-like snout, the Little Freetail Bat has a flattened head and body enabling it to hide in small cracks and crevices, soft fur, grey to brownish-grey above and paler below. It has large triangular ears and a protruding, wrinkled upper lip with a dense fringe of stiff hairs. The feet are stout with fleshy toes fringed with stiff, curled hairs, and the tail projects well beyond the tail-membrane. Studies show that the Little Freetail Bat is actually three different species, although they are yet to be formally named. One has a penis less than 5 mm long, and is restricted to arid and semi arid areas of inland Australia. Two have shaggier, longer fur and a penis more than 9 mm long. One is confined to southwestern WA, the other is found inland of the Great Dividing Range in NSW, Western Vic. and southeastern SA. **Behaviour** Active mainly at night, they fly fast and direct above the forest canopy, sometimes travelling more than 10 km to food sources. They have difficulty taking-off from the ground, and must climb to at least 1 m to launch themselves. They have good sight and can detect insects in complete darkness using echo-location, emitting high-pitched audible calls. They forage in open areas, over creeks and waterholes, and on the ground, scurrying around searching for terrestrial insects, and can swim well if necessary. By day they roost alone or in colonies of 150 or more bats in tree hollows and crevices, under loose bark and in buildings, often sharing roosts with other bat species. **Development** Females are sexually mature in their first year, males in their second year. Males produce mature sperm in late summer and autumn when food is plentiful, and usually mate in late autumn, although they can store viable sperm until the following spring, allowing them to mate throughout the winter. After mating the female stores the sperm until August when she fertilises her ova. A single young is born from November to January and suckles from a teat in the mother's armpit. The young are independent at about 3 months. **Diet** Flying and terrestrial insects, including ants, beetles and flies. **Habitat** Dry sclerophyll forests, woodlands, mallee scrub, grasslands and deserts. **Status** Probably secure. **Head-body** 47-65 mm. **Forearm** 30-40 mm. **Tail** 25-40 mm. **Weight** 7-15 g.

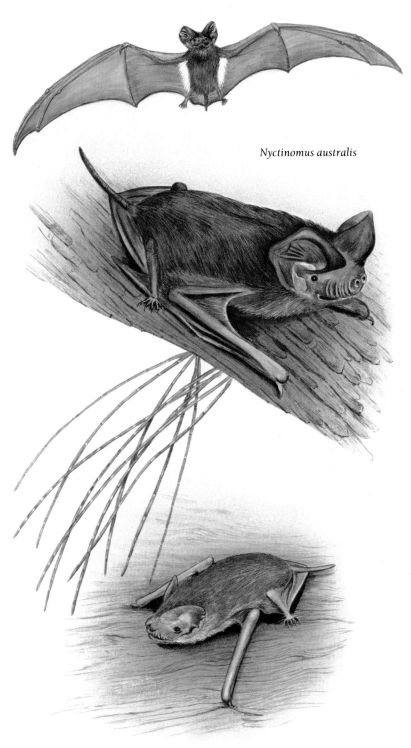

Nyctinomus australis

Mormopterus planiceps

East-coast Freetail Bat

Mormopterus norfolkensis

This tiny bat was mistakenly assumed to come from Norfolk Island, and for many years was known as the Norfolk Island Mastiff Bat. It has an upturned snout and protruding wrinkled upper lip giving it a bulldog-like appearance. The soft fur is dark brownish-grey to reddish-brown above and slightly paler below. It has large triangular ears which are not joined above the head, and males have a neck pouch of unknown function. The feet have thick, fleshy toes fringed with long, stiff, curled hairs, and the tail projects well beyond the tail-membrane. **Behaviour** Active mainly at night, East-coast Freetail Bats roost by day alone or in small colonies in tree hollows and crevices, under loose bark, in caves and buildings. They hunt for insects above the forest canopy and in clearings, flying fast and direct but with limited manoeuvrability. They have good sight, and are able to detect flying insects in the dark using echo-location, emitting high-pitched calls. They also forage on the ground, scurrying around searching for terrestrial insects. **Development** The development of East-coast Freetail Bats has not been studied. Like other freetail bats they probably give birth to a single young that suckles from a teat in the mother's armpit. **Diet** Flying and terrestrial insects. **Habitat** Sclerophyll forests, woodlands and occasionally rainforests. **Status** Probably secure, but very sparse. **Head-body** 45-55 mm. **Tail** 30-45 mm. **Forearm** 35-40 mm. **Weight** 6-10 g.

Beccari's Freetail Bat

Mormopterus beccarii

Often confused with the Little Freetail Bat, this species is larger and found in tropical Australia. Beccari's Freetail Bat is a robust, muscular, insectivorous bat with thick, elastic flight membranes and short, narrow, pointed wings. A large wrinkled upper lip fringed with stiff hairs and furrowed cheeks give it a bulldog-like appearance. It has a flattened head and body and hides in small cracks and crevices. The soft fur is dark grey-brown above and paler below. The large triangular ears are not joined above the head. The feet are stout with fleshy toes fringed with stiff curled hairs. The tail projects well beyond the tail-membrane. **Behaviour** Active mainly at night, Beccari's Freetail Bats roost by day in colonies of up to 50 bats in tree hollows and crevices, under loose bark and in buildings. They emerge at dusk and fly fast and direct with little manoeuvrability, hunting for insects above the forest canopy, along watercourses and over water. They use echo-location to detect insects in the dark, emitting high-pitched calls and homing in on flying insects up to 10 m away. They also have good sight and glean plant-eating bugs from the foliage and scurry around on the ground searching for flightless insects. **Development** Females give birth to a single young in the summer wet season. Pregnant females have been recorded from October to January and lactating females from November to January. The newborn suckles from a teat in the mother's armpit. **Diet** Flying and terrestrial insects, including beetles, moths, flies and grasshoppers. **Habitat** Wet and dry sclerophyll forests, woodlands, rainforests and urban areas. **Status** Secure **Head-body** 54-65 mm. **Tail** 21-38 mm. **Forearm** 35-41 mm. **Weight** 10-19 g.

Mormopterus norfolkensis

Mormopterus beccarii

Lesser Long-eared Bat

Nyctophilus geoffroyi

One of Australia's most widespread bats, the Lesser Long-eared Bat is a tiny insectivorous bat with long fluffy fur, light grey-brown on the back and paler on the belly. It has small eyes, a small low noseleaf with a central Y-shaped groove projecting above the snout. The long, ribbed ears are joined above the head and have a short lower lobe. The tail is enclosed in the tail-membrane. **Behaviour** Active mainly at night, Lesser Long-eared Bats leave their roost just after dark to hunt for insects, travelling 11 km or more overnight. They fly slowly with great manoeuvrability, foraging in the understorey, hovering over leaves, landing to take flightless insects and lifting off vertically from the ground. They have good vision and hearing and combine these senses with echo-location to detect prey in the dark. Tree hollows and crevices beneath loose bark are common roosts, but caves, abandoned bird nests, rocks and buildings are frequently used. They use a number of roost sites in a particular area, usually roosting alone or in groups of 2-3, although colonies of 200 or more have been found. Pregnant females form maternity colonies of about 10-15 bats in spring, sometimes with an adult male, and disperse in autumn when the young are independent. In cold southern areas they hibernate through winter or become torpid during the day to save energy. **Development** Males produce sperm in spring and summer and store it until mating in autumn. Females store the sperm through the winter, fertilising their ova in early spring and giving birth, usually to twins, in September-November. Newborn suckle from teats in the mother's armpits and cling to her until well-furred at about 4 weeks. They are then left at the roost while the mother forages, and are weaned at 6-8 weeks. **Diet** Flying and terrestrial insects, particularly moths. **Habitat** Most habitats except tropical and subtropical rainforests, from sea level to 1600 m. **Status** Secure. **Head-body** 38-50 mm. **Forearm** 30-41 mm. **Tail** 30-50 mm. **Weight** 4-15 g.

Little Northern Freetail Bat

Mormopterus loriae

The Little Northern Freetail Bat is a tiny, insectivorous bat with a very flat head and body, enabling it to hide in small cracks and crevices. It has soft, light brownish-grey fur with a whitish base, and is distinctly paler below with a yellowish throat and chin. It has large rounded ears which are not joined above the head, an upturned, hound-like snout with a protruding wrinkled upper lip fringed with stiff hairs. The feet are stout with fleshy toes fringed with stiff curled hairs. The tail projects well beyond the tail-membrane. The western form of this bat is now regarded as a distinct species, and is yet to be named. **Behaviour** Active mainly at night, Little Northern Freetail Bats roost by day alone or in colonies of several hundred bats in tree hollows and crevices, under loose bark, in caves and buildings. They emerge at dusk to hunt for flying insects above and beside the forest canopy, over creeks and waterholes, and on the ground where they scurry around searching for terrestrial insects. They have short, narrow and pointed wings, enabling them to fly fast and direct but with limited manoeuvrability. Prey is detected in the dark by echo-location using high-pitched calls. They also have good sight and hearing. **Development** Females give birth to a single young in the summer wet season which suckles from a teat in the mother's armpit, until weaned around March. **Diet** Flying and terrestrial insects, including beetles and ants. **Habitat** Rainforests, mangroves, monsoon forests, vine thickets, sclerophyll forests, paperbark forests and woodlands. **Status** Probably secure. **Head-body** 42-55 mm. **Tail** 26-40 mm. **Forearm** 28-35 mm. **Weight** 6-10 g.

Nyctophilus geoffroyi

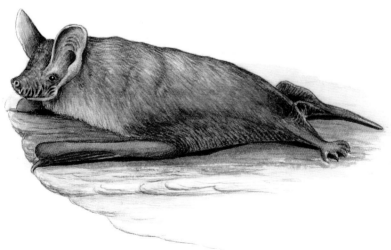

Mormopterus loriae

Gould's Long-eared Bat

Nyctophilus gouldi

Gould's Long-eared Bat used to be considered a subspecies of the Greater Long-eared Bat (*Nyctophilus timorensis*), which it closely resembles, although it is smaller. Their ranges overlap, but Gould's Long-eared Bat prefers wetter, more forested habitats. It is slate-grey to grey-brown above and ash-grey below, mottled with light-buff. It has small eyes, long, ribbed ears joined above the head with a short, broad, triangular lower lobe partially covering the ear aperture. A poorly-developed noseleaf forms a ridge behind the nostrils. The tail is enclosed in the tail-membrane.

Behaviour Active mainly after dusk and in the early morning, their broad wings allow them to fly slowly with great manoeuvrability. They forage in the understorey, taking insects on the wing and gleaning insects from the foliage and the ground, catching prey in their wings, tail membrane or mouth. They have good vision and combine this with hearing and echo-location to navigate and detect insects, usually staying within 2 km of the roost. They roost alone or in colonies of up to 20 in tree hollows and under loose bark, preferring large trees, often changing roosts daily within a group of trees. In southern areas they spend the colder months in torpor, arousing to forage on warmer nights. Females form maternity colonies and before leaving the roost lactating mothers mark their young by smearing them with a yellow liquid secreted from glands on the muzzle, and rub faces with them on return. Females also use social calls to identify and maintain close bonding with their young for the first 3-4 months. **Development** Females are sexually active at 7-9 months, males at 12-15 months. Males produce sperm in summer and store it until mating in April-June. Females store the sperm and fertilise their ova in September-October, giving birth to 1-2 young in October-December. Newborn suckle from teats in the mother's armpits and cling to her for the first 3-5 days while she forages at night, and are then left in the roost. They are born naked, are fully furred by 10 days, begin to fly at 4 weeks and are weaned at 6 weeks. **Diet** Moths, other insects and spiders. **Habitat** Tall wet (and occasionally dry) sclerophyll forests, woodlands and subtropical rainforests, to at least 1250 m. **Status** Secure. **Head-body** 50-70 mm. **Forearm** 34-48 mm. **Tail** 40-60 mm. **Weight** 5-17 g.

Northern Long-eared Bat

Nyctophilus bifax

The Northern Long-eared Bat is a small insectivorous bat with light-brown or tawny-brown fur above and greyish-brown fur below. It has a foreshortened head with relatively large eyes and long ribbed ears, each with a short, broadly triangular lower lobe partially covering the ear aperture. A poorly-developed noseleaf forms a low ridge behind the nostrils. The tail is enclosed in the tail-membrane.

Behaviour Active mainly at night, Northern Long-eared Bats roost by day in tree hollows, under peeling bark, among epiphytes and dense foliage, emerging at dusk to hunt for insects in the forest understorey. Their broad wings allow them to fly slowly with high manoeuvrability and to hover and take off from the ground. They usually hang from trees 5-10 m high, rotate back and forth and make short flights every few minutes to catch insects in flight, glean them from the foliage or from the ground. They have good vision and use low-intensity echo-location calls to navigate and detect insects in the dark. Individuals often roost communally and move from summer roosts near the rainforest edge to warmer winter roosts deep in the forest. **Development** They mate in May and females usually give birth to twins in October. Newborn suckle from teats in the mother's armpits and are carried clinging to her fur while she forages for the first few days. They are then left at the maternity roost until weaned and able to hunt. Females often move their young to different roost sites. **Diet** Flying and terrestrial insects. **Habitat** Tropical rainforests, paperbark forests to dry sclerophyll forests and woodlands, often near watercourses. **Status** Probably secure. **Head-body** 35-56 mm. **Tail** 34-46 mm. **Forearm** 32-46 mm. **Weight** 6-14 g.

Nyctophilus gouldi

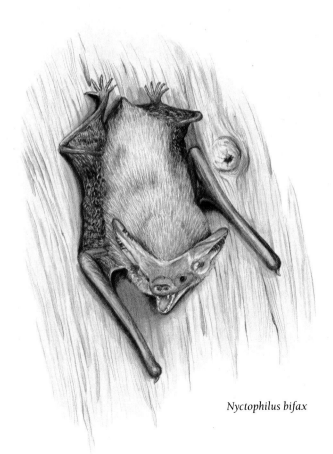

Nyctophilus bifax

Common Bentwing Bat

Miniopterus schreibersii

One of the world's most widely distributed mammals, the Common Bentwing Bat is so-named because the exceptionally long tip of its third finger bends under the wing at rest. The fur is chocolate-brown above and paler below. Patches of bright-rufous fur appear during the annual moult, and old bats are gingerish. The forehead is high and well-furred, the muzzle short. The tail is enclosed in the tail-membrane and folded under the body at rest. **Behaviour** Nocturnal, they fly fast and direct at up to 50 kph, making sudden dives to take small flying insects, generally hunting above the forest canopy, and travelling up to 70 km overnight. They have good vision and combine this with echo-location and hearing to detect insects in the dark. They roost in caves, mine tunnels and buildings, hanging from the roof or walls in separate massed clusters of the same sex or age group. Populations use the same roosts every year. Both sexes congregate in spring, and pregnant females join colonies of up to 150,000 bats in warm, humid, maternity caves, which may be up to 250 km from their springtime roosts, where they raise their young. Colonies disperse in February and March, and individual bats migrate to winter roosts. In cold climates they become torpid for long periods to save energy. **Development** Females become sexually active in their second year. They mate in September in tropical regions and May-June in temperate regions (although the embryo remains dormant over winter). A single, naked young is born in December-January (6 weeks earlier in South Australia), and suckles from a teat in the mother's armpit. Young are left in clusters on the cave roof while the mother forages. They can fly at 7 weeks, reach adult size at 10 weeks, and may live to 18 years or more. **Diet** Moths and other flying insects. **Habitat** Prefers forested valleys, but utilises many habitats, including grasslands. **Status** Probably secure, but vulnerable in NSW where few suitable maternity caves and overwintering sites remain. **Head-body** 47-63 mm. **Forearm** 43-51 mm. **Tail** 50-60 mm. **Weight** 9-20 g.

Little Bentwing Bat

Miniopterus australis

The Little Bentwing Bat is so-named because the tip of its third finger (which supports the tip of the wing membrane) is exceptionally long and bends under the wing at rest. The fur is greyish-black to fawn-brown above and paler below. It moults early in the year, and the fur gradually becomes browner. The forehead is high and well-furred, and the muzzle is short. The tail is enclosed in the tail-membrane and folded under the body at rest. **Behaviour** Little Bentwing Bats are active at night and roost by day in caves, mine tunnels, tree hollows and buildings, hanging from the roof or walls and often forming mixed clusters with Common Bentwing Bats, particularly in the south. Colonies of up to 100,000 or more congregate in early spring. Most adult males and juveniles disperse in summer, leaving maternity colonies of females and their young in warm nursery caves. In southern areas they move into cool overwintering caves and become torpid to save energy. They have good vision and use echo-location to navigate and detect insects in the dark, flying quickly with great manoeuvrability, hunting for flying insects in densely wooded areas between the understorey and forest canopy. **Development** Mating takes place in July or August and a single young is born in December. Newborn suckle from a teat in the mother's armpit until weaned in February. Very young bats are left in massed clusters in the maternity cave while the mother forages at night. They have a potential lifespan of more than 5 years. **Diet** Flying insects. **Habitat** Wet and dry sclerophyll forests, paperbark swamps and rainforests. **Status** Vulnerable, threatened by mining and disturbance of nursery caves and overwintering sites. **Head-body** 40-48 mm. **Tail** 39-48 mm. **Forearm** 36-40 mm. **Weight** 5-8 g.

Miniopterus schreibersii

Miniopterus australis

Arnhem Land Long-eared Bat
Nyctophilus arnhemensis

A small, tropical, insectivorous bat, the Arnhem Land Long-eared Bat is olive-brown to light-brown above and pale-brown to greyish-brown below, with a dark base to the fur. The head is foreshortened with relatively large eyes, long, ribbed ears each with a short, broadly-triangular lower lobe, and a poorly-developed noseleaf forming a low ridge behind the nostrils. The tail is enclosed in the tail-membrane. **Behaviour** Active mainly at night, Arnhem Land Long-eared Bats roost by day in tree hollows, under the loose bark of paperbark trees, amongst foliage and in buildings. They emerge at dusk, their broad wings allowing them to fly slowly and flutteringly with high manoeuvrability as they forage in the forest understorey and over water for flying insects. They also glean flightless insects from the foliage and the ground. They have good vision and use echo-location to navigate and detect insects in the dark. **Development** Little is known about their development. Females give birth to 1-2 young from October to February. Newborn suckle from teats in the mother's armpits. **Diet** Flying and terrestrial insects. **Habitat** Tropical rainforests, mangroves, woodlands and wet sclerophyll forests with an annual rainfall exceeding 500 mm. **Status** Probably secure. **Head-body** 40-59 mm. **Tail** 35-43 mm. **Forearm** 35-40 mm. **Weight** 6-8 g.

Gould's Wattled Bat
Chalinolobus gouldi

Able to exploit a wide range of roosting sites, Gould's Wattled Bat is found in most of Australia. It has soft, dense fur, dark chocolate-brown to black above, often grading to brown towards the rump, and slightly lighter below. The muzzle is short and the forehead high. The ears are short and broad with a loose flap hanging down at the corner of the mouth, and a prominent rounded lobe partially covering the ear aperture. The tail is enclosed in the tail-membrane. **Behaviour** Active from dusk to dawn, Gould's Wattled Bats take insects in flight or from the foliage, utilising open spaces beneath the canopy. They forage up to 15 km from their roost site, flying fast and direct, with sudden zig-zag changes of course, on long, narrow wings. Roosts are in tree hollows, under loose bark, in rock crevices and buildings. Males are generally solitary, but females form colonies of 8-40 bats (200 have been recorded in a building), and individuals move frequently between roost sites in a particular area. Most juveniles disperse within 3 months of independence. In cold climates when food is scarce they become torpid to save energy, and in Tasmania they hibernate from late autumn to early spring. They have good sight and combine this with acute hearing and echo-location to detect insects in the dark, emitting an audible high-pitched sound in flight. Other vocalisations include buzzes, squeaks and chirps. **Development** Females are able to breed in their first year and mate at the beginning of winter, although the sperm is stored until they ovulate at the end of winter. Twins are born from September to October in the north and in late November in the south, and attach to teats in the mother's armpit. They grow rapidly, reaching adult size in one month, and are carried by the mother until well-furred, when they are left at the roost while she forages. The young are independent at 6 weeks, and may live to 5 years or more. **Diet** A wide range of flying and crawling insects. **Habitat** Most habitats from urban areas, to deserts, tropical forests and alpine regions to 1500 m. **Status** Secure. **Head-body** 46-60 mm. **Forearm** 35-50 mm. **Tail** 31-50 mm. **Weight** 6-20 g.

Nyctophilus arnhemensis

Chalinolobus gouldi

Chocolate Wattled Bat

Chalinolobus morio

The Chocolate Wattled Bat is an insectivorous bat with soft, dense, chocolate-brown fur, and small wattles at the corner of its mouth. It has small eyes, a short muzzle and a high forehead with a ridge of fur between the eyes and snout. The ears are relatively small and rounded with a small lobe at the inner base. The tail protrudes slightly beyond the edge of the tail-membrane. **Behaviour** Active between dusk and dawn, Chocolate Wattled Bats fly fast between the tree canopy and understorey, sweeping low over forest trails hunting for insects. They have long, narrow wings and fly fast and direst with good manoeuvrability, dropping suddenly on prey. They roost in tree hollows, abandoned bird nests, rock crevices, buildings and caves. Males usually roost alone, while females form colonies of up to several hundred bats, staying within a home range of up to 5 km. In cold climates they hibernate when food is short, entering hibernation later and emerging earlier than other small forest bats to take advantage of food resources. They have good sight, acute hearing and use echo-location to detect insects in the dark. **Development** Males produce sperm in spring and summer and store it until mating in autumn. The female stores this sperm until ovulation and fertilisation in late winter, giving birth to 1-2 naked young in October in Queensland and November in southern areas. Newborn suckle from teats in the mother's armpits, are carried until well-furred and become independent in January or February. **Diet** Flying insects, mainly moths and beetles. **Habitat** Wet and dry sclerophyll forests, rainforests, dry scrub and woodlands, to about 1600 m. **Status** Secure. **Head-body** 49-61 mm. **Forearm** 34-43 mm. **Tail** 39-50 mm. **Weight** 5-14 g.

Hoary Bat

Chalinolobus nigrogriseus

A small insectivorous bat, the Hoary Bat takes its name from the white tips of its blackish-grey fur, which give it a frosted or hoary appearance. It has a foreshortened head with small eyes, a high forehead, relatively short, rounded ears with a small horizontal lobe between the bottom of the ear and the mouth. The tail is enclosed in the tail-membrane. **Behaviour** Active mainly at night, Hoary Bats roost by day in tree hollows and rock crevices. They are among the first bats to emerge from the roost after sunset, flying moderately fast and direct, hunting close to the ground in clearings, over small water bodies or above the tree canopy. They are very manoeuvrable, deviating suddenly from their flight path to catch evasive insects on the wing. Insects are also gleaned from the foliage and from the ground. They have good sight and use echo-location in the dark to navigate and detect insects up to 5 m away. **Development** Little is known about their development. Females probably give birth to 1-2 young from October to November. Newborn suckle from teats in the mother's armpits, and are weaned by January. **Diet** Moths, flies, beetles, crickets, spiders, ants and other invertebrates. **Habitat** Wet sclerophyll forests, monsoon forests, vine thickets, rainforests, woodlands, heath, coastal scrub and sand dunes. **Status** Probably secure. **Head-body** 39-48 mm. **Tail** 29-39 mm. **Forearm** 30-40 mm. **Weight** 4-10 g.

Chalinolobus morio

Chalinolobus nigrogriseus

Northern Broad-nosed Bat

Scotorepens sanborni

The Northern Broad-nosed Bat is often found in roof spaces, and becomes aggressive if handled. It is a small, slender, insectivorous bat with long, soft, brown fur, tinged with red above and paler below. It has a broad head with a squarish outline when seen from above, a low forehead, small eyes, broadly rounded ears with a narrow pointed lobe partially covering the aperture, a sparsely-haired muzzle with glandular swellings and only two upper incisor teeth. The tail is enclosed in the tail-membrane. **Behaviour** Active at night and soon after sunset, Northern Broad-nosed Bats roost by day in tree hollows and buildings. They roost with 10-20 other bats in tree hollows, although several hundred may congregate in roof buildings. They are one of the first bats to emerge after sunset, flying fast with much diving and darting to catch insects. They hunt in the forest understorey, above watercourses, around calm coastal bays and urban street lights. They are often seen in summer skimming over still freshwater lakes and ponds, dipping their mouth in to drink, and seldom fly more than 5 m above the ground. They have good sight and use echo-location to navigate and detect their prey. **Development** Little is known about their development. They probably mate in May or June and give birth to a single young in late September or October which suckles from a teat in the mother's armpit. **Diet** Mosquitos, midges, mayflies and other flying insects. **Habitat** Monsoon forests, rainforests, woodlands, mangroves and heathlands. **Status** Probably secure. **Head-body** 36-52 mm. **Tail** 27-39 mm. **Forearm** 27-36 mm. **Weight** 5-9 g. Females are usually larger than males.

Large Pied Bat

Chalinolobus dwyeri

The Large Pied Bat is an insectivorous bat with velvety, glossy-black fur and a white V-shaped stripe in the pubic region beneath the wings and tail membrane. It has small eyes, a high forehead and a short muzzle with glandular swellings. The ears are moderately large with a broad rounded lobe covering the base of the ear aperture, and a horizontal lobe extending from the base towards the corner of the mouth. The tail is enclosed in the tail-membrane. **Behaviour** Active at night and after sunset, Large Pied Bats roost by day on the ceilings of caves in the twilight zone near the entrance, in mine tunnels and sometimes in the abandoned, bottle-shaped mud nests of Fairy Martins. Small mixed colonies congregate in early spring, huddling together for warmth. Individuals leave the colonies in late autumn, and in the southern part of their range they become torpid or hibernate during the coldest months to conserve energy when food is scarce. They have short, broad wings, fly fairly slowly with moderate manoeuvrability and hunt for small flying insects below the forest canopy. They have good sight and use echo-location to navigate and detect insects in the dark. Males secrete a milky substance from glands on either side of the muzzle during the breeding season **Development** Females become sexually mature at about 12 months and give birth to 1-2 young in late November or early December. Newborn suckle from teats in the mother's armpits, are weaned in late January and are independent by late February. **Diet** Flying insects. **Habitat** Dry sclerophyll forests and woodlands to about 1500 m. **Status** Vulnerable; threatened by logging and land clearing. **Head-body** 45-55 mm. **Tail** 40-47 mm. **Forearm** 38-42 mm. **Weight** 7-10 g.

Scotorepens sanborni

Chalinolobus dwyeri

Greater Broad-nosed Bat

Scoteanax rueppellii

The Greater Broad-nosed Bat preys on insects and at least 8 other bat species. It has long, soft fur, dark reddish-brown to dark-brown above and slightly paler below. Its broad head has a squarish outline when viewed from above, a low forehead, small eyes, broadly rounded ears with a narrow, pointed lobe partially covering the ear aperture. The muzzle is sparsely-haired with glandular swellings, and only 2 upper incisor teeth are present, distinguishing it from the externally similar Great Pipistrelle (which occurs in the same area and has 4 upper incisors). The tail is enclosed in the tail-membrane. **Behaviour** Active from dusk to dawn, Greater Broad-nosed Bats are one of the first bats to emerge just after sunset. Their flight is slow and direct, and they hunt about 3-6 m above the ground, making only slight deviations from their flight path to catch moths, beetles and other large, slow-flying insects. They forage in forests and woodlands, utilising openings in the forest and corridors above creeks and small rivers, hawking back and forth looking for prey, taking small animals from the ground and foliage. They have good sight and use echo-location to navigate and detect prey in the dark, which sometimes includes other small bats and mice. They roost by day in tree hollows and the roof spaces of abandoned buildings. Pregnant females congregate at maternity sites in suitable trees where they give birth and raise their young, apparently excluding males. **Development** Little is known about their development. A single young is born in January and suckles from a teat in the mother's armpit. **Diet** Insects, bats, mice and other small vertebrates. **Habitat** Sclerophyll forests, rainforests, woodlands and moist gullies below 500 m in the south and 800 m in the north. **Status** Probably secure, but rare and sparsely distributed. **Head-body** 63-95 mm. **Tail** 40-59 mm. **Forearm** 50-56 mm. **Weight** 20-35 g.

Large-footed Mouse-eared Bat

Myotis adversus

A small coastal bat with unusual foraging and social behaviour, the Large-footed Mouse-eared Bat is grey-brown to dark-brown above, slightly paler on the belly and frosted with silver-grey on the chest. Older bats become ginger. Albinism and partial albinism are frequently seen. The ears are large and funnel-shaped with a long, pointed lobe partially covering the aperture. The feet are large with sharp, curved claws and a very long ankle bone. The tail is enclosed in the tail-membrane. Recent studies have divided this species into 3 species in Australia, but they have not yet been clarified. **Behaviour** Active mainly at night, Large-footed Mouse-eared Bats often hunt in small groups near the banks of rivers or lakes, flying slowly with great manoeuvrability, spiralling downward to catch flying insects. They also rake aquatic insects and small fish from the water with their large clawed feet, or scoop them up with their tail membrane. Prey is detected using a combination of good eyesight, acute hearing and echo-location. They roost close to freshwater in caves, tunnels, buildings, tree hollows, among dense foliage and pandanus leaves. Colonies generally comprise 10-15 bats, but 200 have been recorded. In the breeding season adult males defend a tiny exclusive roosting site and control a harem of up to 12 females; older males have scarred ears from fighting. In southern areas they become torpid for periods during winter. **Development** Sexual activity begins in the first year of life. A single litter is produced in November-December in the south. In subtropical regions at least 2 litters are produced in early October and late January, while in the tropics 3 successive litters may be produced in one year. The single young suckles for about 8 weeks from a teat in the mother's armpit, and remains with her until independent 3-4 weeks later. **Diet** Insects and small fish. **Habitat** Sclerophyll forests, mangroves, paperbark swamps, woodlands and rainforests near slow-flowing creeks, lakes and estuaries. **Status** Probably secure, but vulnerable in NSW. **Head-body** 35-60 mm. **Forearm** 36-43 mm. **Tail** 33-42 mm. **Weight** 5-12 g.

Scoteanax rueppellii

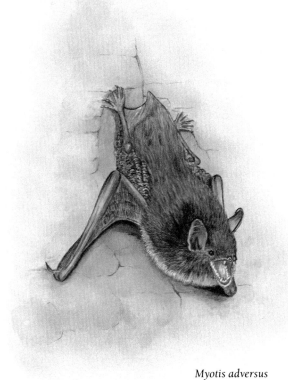

Myotis adversus

Little Broad-nosed Bat

Scotorepens greyii

Widely distributed in hot, arid habitats, the Little Broad-nosed Bat is an aggressive insectivorous bat with long, soft fur, chestnut to grey-brown or ginger above, and paler below. It has a broad head with a low forehead and a squarish outline when viewed from above, small eyes, broadly rounded ears with a rounded lobe partially covering the aperture, a sparsely-haired muzzle with glandular swellings, and slightly protruding nostrils. The tail protrudes slightly from the tail-membrane.
Behaviour Active at night and soon after sunset, Little Broad-nosed Bats roost by day in tree hollows, hollow fence posts and abandoned buildings, in pairs or colonies of up to 20 bats. Daily access to water is essential in the hot, arid interior. They emerge at dusk and forage for flying and terrestrial insects in woodlands and plains mostly over waterholes and creeks. Prey is detected by a combination of good eyesight and echo-location. They fly quickly, darting frequently to catch insects, taking occasional drinks by skimming over the surface of still water. **Development** Mating probably takes place in April, before the onset of winter in southern districts, with females giving birth in October and November, usually to twins. Mating may occur later in the tropics. Newborn suckle from teats in the mother's armpits and are able to fly by mid-December. **Diet** Moths, flies, beetles, crickets, ants and termites. **Habitat** Wet and dry sclerophyll forests, monsoon forests, paperbark forests, woodlands, arid areas, sand dunes and plains. **Status** Common. **Head-body** 37-55 mm. **Tail** 25-49 mm. **Forearm** 27-35 mm. **Weight** 4-12 g.

Inland Broad-nosed Bat

Scotorepens balstoni

The Inland Broad-nosed Bat is an insectivorous bat found over much of the arid and semi-arid regions of Australia. It is grey to grey-brown or chestnut-brown above and pale-brown below. It has a broad head with a low forehead, a wide, sparsely-haired muzzle with glandular swellings, slightly protruding nostrils and a V-shaped cleft in the lower lip. The eyes are small and the ears broadly rounded with a short, rounded lobe partially covering the aperture. The tail is enclosed in the tail-membrane and is arched under the body at rest and in flight. **Behaviour** Active soon after sunset, they fly relatively slowly, with rapid diversions, only reacting to insects closer than 2 m. They forage below the canopy and at the edge of forests, skim repeatedly over water to catch small flying insects, and glean insects from the foliage and the ground. They have good sight and combine this with acute hearing and echo-location to detect prey. They roost in tree hollows, crevices and abandoned buildings, forming small colonies of up to 45 bats, often sharing roosts with larger colonies of the Little Freetail Bat. Pregnant females form maternity colonies. **Development** Mating takes place in April-May in the south and in September in the north. Females give birth to 1-2 young in October-November. Newborn are naked but well developed and able to walk. They suckle from teats in the mother's armpits, clinging to her for the first 10 days of life until they are too heavy to be carried. They are then left in the roost while she forages, and are independent at 5 weeks of age. **Diet** Insects including mosquitoes, termites, beetles, crickets, moths, flies and ants. **Habitat** Dry forests, woodlands, mallee scrub and farmlands, near permanent water. **Status** Probably secure; widespread but uncommon. **Head-body** 42-60 mm. **Forearm** 30-41 mm. **Tail** 29-42 mm. **Weight** 6-14 g.

Scotorepens greyii

Scotorepens balstoni

Eastern False Pipistrelle

Falsistrellus tasmaniensis

The Eastern False Pipistrelle is a relatively large insectivorous bat with long, soft fur, rich-brown to reddish-brown above and slightly paler below. It has small eyes, a short, sparsely-haired muzzle with glandular swellings on the sides, long narrow ears with rounded tips, a notch on the outer edge and a narrow, sharply-pointed lobe partially covering the aperture. It has a long tail that protrudes slightly beyond the tail-membrane. **Behaviour** Active mainly at night, Eastern False Pipistrelles fly fast and direct with limited manoeuvrability, foraging above or just below the tree canopy, up to 12 km from their roost. They attack insects on the wing by sudden changes in course, rather than by acrobatic movements. They have good sight, acute hearing and the ability to pin-point insects using echo-location. Tree hollows, caves and sometimes abandoned buildings are used for roosts, and they usually form single-sex colonies of 3-36 bats. In cooler mainland areas they migrate from the highlands to warmer coastal areas in winter, and in Tasmania they appear to hibernate from late autumn to early spring. **Development** Males produce sperm in the late summer or autumn when food supplies are plentiful, store it through the colder months and mate in late spring and early summer. A single young is born in December and suckles from a teat in the mother's armpit. **Diet** Moths, beetles, bugs, ants, flies and other insects. **Habitat** Wet forests and woodlands, preferring gullies and highland areas up to 1500 m. **Status** Vulnerable; threatened by land clearing. **Head-body** 55-70 mm. **Forearm** 45-56 mm. **Tail** 40-51 mm. **Weight** 14-29 g.

Northern Pipistrelle

Pipistrellus westralis

A tiny bat with a delicate body, the Northern Pipistrelle is sometimes seen in urban areas in northern Australia catching flying insects around street lamps. It is dark-brown to black above and lighter below. The head has a flattened crown and a sparsely-haired muzzle with glandular swellings on the sides. The ears are broadly triangular with rounded tips and have a triangular lobe partially covering the aperture. The upper jaw has two incisor teeth almost equal in length with slight indentations. The tail is enclosed in the tail-membrane. **Behaviour** Active mainly at night, Northern Pipistrelles roost by day in tree hollows and crevices, among dead palm fronds, below the leaf bases of pandans, in mines, caves and under house roofs. They land upright and turn over to hang by their feet or cling to vertical surfaces. They emerge after sunset to hunt for insects, following the outer foliage of the forest, flying below the canopy and around mangrove communities. They have a fast, fluttering flying pattern, swerving rapidly to take flying insects detected by sight or by echo-location in the dark. **Development** Northern Pipistrelles breed year round. Females give birth to a single young that suckles from a teat in the mother's armpit. **Diet** Moths, beetles and other flying insects. **Habitat** Mangroves, pandan thickets, paperbark swamps, and urban areas in coastal and near-coastal sites. **Status** Probably secure. **Head-body** 34-43 mm. **Tail** 29-37 mm. **Forearm** 27-31 mm. **Weight** 2.7-3.3 g.

Falsistrellus tasmaniensis

Pipistrellus westralis

Large Forest Bat

Vespadelus darlingtoni

The Large Forest Bat is a small, insectivorous bat with long, dark-brown to rusty-red fur, with a brown base and light-brown or grey tips, becoming very dark-brown to black in older animals. It has dark-brown to black wings, an abrupt forehead, rounded ears with a narrow lobe partially covering the aperture, and a membrane enclosing the tail. **Behaviour** Active mainly at night, Large Forest Bats fly fast and direct, making sudden gliding manoeuvres to attack flying insects. They hunt in open spaces below the forest canopy and around the top of the understorey, locating prey by echo-location, acute vision and hearing. They roost in tree hollows, under loose bark, in crevices and abandoned buildings, alone, in groups of 5-6 or in colonies of up to 80 bats. Pregnant females form maternity colonies, often cohabiting with other bat species. In colder climates they hibernate from late autumn to early spring, emerging to feed on warm days when insects are abroad. **Development** Males produce sperm in spring and summer and store it until they mate in autumn. Females store the sperm over winter and use it to fertilise their ova in early spring. A single young is born in November-December and suckles from a teat in the mother's armpit. The mother carries the young while she forages until it becomes too heavy when it is left at the roost. Young become independent in January-February. Females become sexually mature in their first year, males in their second year. **Diet** Moths and other flying insects. **Habitat** Wet and dry sclerophyll forests and woodlands, rainforests, alpine moors, often near lakes, to about 1300 m. **Status** Secure. **Head-body** 38-50 mm. **Forearm** 31-37 mm. **Tail** 29-40 mm. **Weight** 6-10 g.

Little Forest Bat

Vespadelus vulturnus

The Little Forest Bat is a small insectivorous bat with dark to mid-grey fur on its back, sometimes tinged with brown, and a grey belly sometimes flecked with white. The skin on the upper forearms is lighter grey than on the wing membranes. It has a high forehead, a small furred muzzle and rounded ears with a narrow, translucent-white lobe partially covering the aperture. The tail is enclosed in the tail-membrane. **Behaviour** Active mainly at night, Little Forest Bats hunt for flying insects below the forest canopy in the upper levels of the understorey, alighting at a perch to eat larger insects. Their flight is fast and fluttering with rapid changes of direction and spiralling dives to catch insects. Prey is located using echo-location, acute hearing and eyesight, and is sometimes caught in the wing or tail membrane. They roost in tree hollows and abandoned buildings, alone or in colonies of up to 70 bats, hanging from the walls or the backs of other bats. Females form separate maternity colonies in early summer and mate with visiting males soon after giving birth. They disperse to mixed-sex winter roosts in late autumn, and become torpid for long periods in winter. **Development** Females are sexually mature in their first year, males in their second year of life. Mating takes place from March to the end of winter. Females store sperm until spring when ovulation and fertilisation occur. A single young is born in November or December and suckles for about 6 weeks from a teat in the mother's armpit. It is carried while she forages until it becomes too heavy, when it is then left at the roost until becoming independent at about 9 weeks of age. **Diet** A wide range of flying insects. **Habitat** Wet and dry sclerophyll forests and woodlands, mainly below 400 m, with patchy distribution to 1100 m. **Status** Secure. **Head-body** 34-50 mm. **Forearm** 24-33 mm. **Tail** 27-35 mm. **Weight** 3-7 g.

Vespadelus darlingtoni

Vespadelus vulturnus

Water-rat

Hydromys chrysogaster

A Rabbit-size placental mammal, the Water-rat is the largest Australian rodent. It has soft, dense, water-repellent fur varying from dark-grey to black or brown above, and white, cream or golden-yellow below, with a white-tipped tail. The body is streamlined for swimming with a flattened head, long, blunt muzzle, small eyes and ears and a thick tail used as a rudder. The hindfeet are large and broad with webbing between the toes. They have one pair of upper and lower gnawing incisor teeth, but unlike other rodents have only 2 molars on each side of the lower jaw. **Behaviour** Active mainly at night, Water-rats also forage in the early morning and evening. They sleep in a nest in a burrow dug into the bank of a waterway, or sometimes in a log. Burrows have a round entrance about 15 cm across, hidden in vegetation, run parallel to the bank, and have one or more inner nest chambers some 20 cm high. Water-rats are solitary except when mating or with young, and fight to establish dominance hierarchies and defend territories of 2-10 ha or larger. Sluggish on land, they follow tracks along the water's edge to feeding sites, stalk through vegetation for prey and dive around likely food sources, often emerging some distance away, carrying their catch to a favourite feeding platform. **Development** Sexually mature at 4-8 months, they continue to grow throughout their life of 3-4 years. Breeding occurs year-round with peaks in late winter and spring, and most young are born from September to February. They rear 1-5 litters annually of usually 3-4 young, born 34 days after mating. Females have 4 teats and suckle their young in the nest for about 4 weeks. They are independent at about 8 weeks and moult twice a year. **Diet** Fish, crustaceans, molluscs, frogs, water birds, eggs, bats and aquatic insects. **Habitat** Close to fresh, brackish or saltwater wetlands, creeks, rivers and estuaries, with good vegetative cover, to about 1500 m. **Traces** Scats, shells and other remains near feeding platforms. Scats are up to 10 mm across and 20-25 mm long, containing coarse fragments of shells, scales and bones. **Status** Probably secure; protected in Vic. **Head-body** 230-370 mm. **Tail** 225-330 mm. **Weight** 340-1280 g.

Giant White-tailed Rat

Uromys caudimaculatus

A Rabbit-size placental mammal, the Giant White-tailed Rat is one of Australia's largest rodents. It has coarse fur with long spiny guard hairs, grey-brown above and creamy-white below, with pale paws. The tail is almost naked with non-overlapping scales; the terminal third is white, the remainder is dark-grey mottled with white patches. The muzzle is long with many black whiskers. The eyes and ears are small. The limbs are short with large, strongly-clawed hindfeet. It has one pair of upper and lower gnawing incisor teeth and 3 pairs of molars on each side of the jaw. **Behaviour** Active mainly at night, Giant White-tailed Rats sleep by day in tree hollows or burrows under fallen logs or stream banks, lined with vegetation. They are found alone or in pairs, and have overlapping home ranges of 4 ha or more. Males are very aggressive to other males during the breeding season and emit harsh threatening growls. Fast and agile climbers, they forage on the ground and in trees, using their semi-prehensile tail to grip branches, bounding up trees, gripping with their forefeet and pushing with their strong hindlegs. Their jaws are able to break hard-shelled nuts, which are often taken to a favourite feeding spot on a log or tree buttress. Some seeds are buried near the tree, marked with a leaf, and eaten the following night. Beetles are dug from rotting logs, and bark is eaten. **Development** Sexually mature at about 10 months, they breed from September to January. Females have 4 teats and rear 2-3 young born 36 days after mating. Newborn cling to the teats and may be carried by the mother if she leaves the nest. They suckle for about 5 weeks, are independent at about 2-3 months and may live to 4 years or more. **Diet** Nuts (including coconuts), fruits, insects, fungi, bark, small reptiles, amphibians, crabs and eggs. **Habitat** Wet sclerophyll forests, rainforests, woodlands, mangroves and melaleuca forests. **Traces** Chewed seed cases at feeding sites. Bark torn from buttressed trees. Scats are dark-brown or black, 3-4 mm across and 10-15 mm long, containing fine powdery particles and fragments of insects and scales. **Status** Secure. **Head-body** 275-385 mm. **Tail** 320-362 mm. **Weight** 500-890 g.

Hydromys chrysogaster

Uromys caudimaculatus

Golden-backed Tree-rat

Mesembriomys macrurus

A Rabbit-size placental mammal, the Golden-backed Tree-rat is an arboreal rodent of tropical northern Australia. It has coarse fur, golden-brown on the back, grading to grey on the sides and white below. The base of the long tail is grey, the rest is white with a brushy tip and overlapping scales. The ears are long and rounded, the eyes bulging and the hindfeet broad with strong claws and well-developed sole pads. It has one pair of upper and lower gnawing incisor teeth and three pairs of molars on each side of the jaw. **Behaviour** Active mainly at night, Golden-backed Tree-rats sleep by day in tree hollows and among dense foliage in nests of loosely woven leaves. Although predominantly arboreal, they also feed on the ground and have been seen foraging just after sunrise along the high-tide line of an open beach. They can travel long distances rapidly, scampering through the grass and undergrowth with the tail held high. Pairs of adults and their immature offspring occupy a home range up to 600 m long. **Development** Females are sexually mature at 10 months and they probably breed year round. They have 4 teats and give birth to 1-3 (usually 2) young about 47 days after mating. The young are weaned at 6-7 weeks and are fully grown at 4 months. **Diet** Flowers, fruits, grass, leaves, insects and shellfish. **Habitat** Open forests and woodlands with a grassy or shrubby understorey, mangroves, palm forests, pandanus clumps and vine thickets, in rugged country with more than 600 mm of rain annually. **Status** Vulnerable; threatened by land clearing and pastoral activities. **Head-body** 180-245 mm. **Tail** 290-360 mm. **Weight** 207-330 g.

Black-footed Tree-rat

Mesembriomys gouldii

The Black-footed Tree-rat is a Rabbit-size placental mammal and one of Australia's largest rodents. It has long, coarse and shaggy fur, grey-brown flecked with black above, and creamy-white below. The tail is black with a white brushy tip and overlapping scales. It has long rounded ears, bulging eyes, and broad hindfeet with strong claws and well-developed sole pads. It has one pair of upper and lower gnawing incisor teeth and 3 pairs of molars on each side of the jaw. **Behaviour** Active only at night, Black-footed Tree-rats sleep by day in nests in tree hollows, among palm fronds, in crevices and buildings. They are solitary, and individuals use several nest sites in different trees, preferring hollows about 10 cm diameter and 6-8 m above the ground. They are aggressive and defend their nest sites, uttering threatening grumbling and growling sounds before fighting. They are fast runners and agile climbers and may travel 500 m or more between refuge trees and feeding sites, often feeding on the ground on fallen fruits, rapidly ascending a tree if disturbed. **Development** Black-footed Tree-rats breed throughout the year with a peak in the late dry season (August-September), although few births occur in the wetter months of January-March. Females have 4 teats and usually rear 1-3 young born 43-44 days after mating. Newborn are dragged by the mother clinging to her teats if she leaves the nest until they are fully furred with their eyes open at 10-11 days old. They are weaned at about 28 days and are fully grown at 11-12 weeks. **Diet** Nuts, fruits (including pandanus fruits), flowers, insects and molluscs. **Habitat** Open forests and tropical woodlands with a grassy or shrubby understorey. **Status** Probably secure. **Head-body** 250-310 mm. **Tail** 320-415 mm. **Weight** 580-890 g.

Mesembriomys macrurus

Mesembriomys gouldii

Broad-toothed Rat
Mastacomys fuscus

A stout, thickly-furred rodent of the alps and subalps, the Broad-toothed Rat is named for its unusually broad molar teeth, enabling it to feed on tough plant material. The long fur is light to dark-brown, grading to grey below. The tail is short with small bristles and overlapping scales. The head is wide with rounded ears, and the hindfeet are relatively long and slender. **Behaviour** Although mainly nocturnal, Broad-toothed Rats are often active during the day. They sleep in large, well-insulated nests of finely-shredded grass under logs or dense vegetation, often in button grass. Females have overlapping home ranges up to about 1600 sq m and are very aggressive to males when suckling their young. Males have larger home ranges, up to about 2700 sq m, overlapping those of several females. They nest alone in summer and autumn, and congregate with up to 4 others in communal nests beneath the snow at the beginning of winter. Feeding sites are accessed via tunnels beneath the undergrowth. They stay warm and dry beneath a blanket of snow in winter, and forage even on the coldest days. **Development** Females are sexually mature at about 10 months, and breed from September to February in Tasmania, and December to March in the Snowy Mountains. They have 4 teats and usually produce 2 litters of 1-3 young per season, born about 35 days after mating. Newborn are well-furred, and are dragged behind the mother if she is disturbed, clinging to her teats. They are weaned at about 5 weeks. **Diet** Stems and leaves of grasses and sedges, supplemented with bark, seeds and fungi. **Habitat** Cool, wet, alpine and sub-alpine heaths and sedgelands; coastal grasslands, heaths and woodlands with dense groundcover, to 2200 m. **Traces** Scats are deposited along runways and at nest entrances. They are fibrous, 3-5 mm across and 10-15 mm long, greenish-yellow when fresh and yellow-brown when dry. **Status** Probably secure; vulnerable to land clearing and predation by Cats and Foxes. **Head-body** 140-195 mm. **Tail** 100-135 mm. **Weight** 97-200 g.

Swamp Rat
Rattus lutreolus

A robust, cryptic rodent, the Swamp Rat has long, soft fur, dark-grey to grey-brown above and lighter-grey or buff below. The tail is short, sparsely-haired with overlapping scales. The ears are short and largely concealed by the fur. The feet are dark grey-brown, and the hindfeet are relatively short. Like other rodents they have one pair of upper and lower gnawing incisor teeth and 3 pairs of molars on each side of the jaw. **Behaviour** Although mainly nocturnal, Swamp Rats are frequently active during the day, and sleep in spherical nests of shredded vegetation about 15 cm across, built at the end of a burrow up to 1 m deep, or above ground in tussock grass, rotting logs or hollows in tree bases. Solitary, they are strongly territorial and have small home ranges of about 0.2-0.5 ha. Males increase their home ranges to about 4 ha in the breeding season and roam widely through adjacent female territories searching for mates. Young adults must disperse more than 2 km to establish a new territory. To avoid predators they construct extensive tunnels and runway systems through dense vegetation from their nesting sites to food sources. They can climb and swim fast in emergencies. **Development** Females are sexually mature at about 12 weeks, breed mostly in early spring and summer, and produce several litters of 3-5 young in a good season. Mainland females have 10 teats, while those in Tasmania have only 8 teats. Young are born 21-23 days after mating, are weaned at 3-4 weeks, and live to about 18 months. **Diet** Rhizomes, stems and leaves of sedges and grasses, supplemented by insects, mosses, seeds and fungi. **Habitat** Coastal swamps, river flats, wet heaths, sedgelands, grasslands, woodlands and wet forests with dense, low vegetation, to more than 1000 m altitude. **Traces** Scats are found along runways and nesting sites. They are brown, about 2-5 mm across and 10-15 mm long. **Status** Secure. **Head-body** 120-200 mm. **Tail** 55-150 mm. **Weight** 55-170 g.

Mastacomys fuscus

Rattus lutreolus

Dusky Rat
Rattus colletti

The Dusky Rat lives on the flat, treeless alluvial floodplains of tropical northern Australia. It has long, coarse and spiny fur, grizzled dark-brown to black above, yellowish on the sides and throat, and greyish-buff below. The small ears and long, stout, hairy tail are dark brown. Like other rodents it has one pair of upper and lower gnawing incisor teeth and 3 pairs of molars on each side of the jaw.

Behaviour Dusky Rats modify their lifestyle according to the dramatic seasonal variations of the wet tropics. In the wet season they retreat from rising floodwaters to higher ground and forage at night in shallow water or in the woodlands, sheltering by day beneath tree roots or logs, or in shallow burrows dug into soft soil. As the floodwaters recede they disperse over the drying plains and spend most of their time in crevices in the clay pans foraging for underground sedge corms. Breeding begins at the end of the wet season, and the young are born in nests constructed by the mother in humid crevices. As the dry season progresses they take refuge from the heat in cracks and crevices, and above-ground nocturnal activity stops completely. At this time of year the older animals die. When the rains begin and the cracks in the soil vanish they move out once more to the edge of the plains. **Development** Females are able to breed at about 5 weeks of age. They have 12 teats and give birth to usually 7-9 young, 21-23 days after mating, and wean them at about 20 days. If there is only mild flooding in the wet season, and rain extends into the dry season they will breed throughout the year, although little reproduction takes place in years with extreme weather conditions. **Diet** Grass roots and sedge corms. **Habitat** Coastal floodplains, swamps and tidal rivers fringed with mangroves. **Traces** Scats are pale brown, 2-4 mm wide and about 10 mm long, often curved, containing fine powdery particles. **Status** Secure, with dramatic population fluctuations. **Head-body** 145-210 mm. **Tail** 105-150 mm. **Weight** 85-215 g.

Pale Field-rat
Rattus tunneyi

Usually found in tall grasslands, the Pale Field-rat is an attractive rodent with light shiny yellow-brown fur above and grey or cream fur below. The head is broad and rounded with protruding eyes and short rounded ears. The tail is relatively short and sparsely-haired with overlapping scales. Like other rodents it has one pair of upper and lower gnawing incisor teeth and 3 pairs of molars on each side of the jaw. **Behaviour** Pale Field-rats are strictly nocturnal and spend the day alone or with their offspring in shallow burrow systems dug into loose, sandy soil, or in termite mounds. Burrows have vertical shafts and horizontal tunnels, and often have several entrances marked by large spoil heaps. They appear to live in patchy colonies, and travel between burrows along well-marked runways through the thick grass. Pale Field-rats are docile, curious and easily handled, and will enter houses searching for food. **Development** Females are sexually mature at about 5 weeks. Breeding takes place in spring in NSW, in autumn in Qld and in the dry season in the north. Females have 10 teats and may rear several litters of 2-10 (usually 4-5) young in quick succession. Pregnancy lasts 21-22 days. Young are furred at 7 days, have their eyes open at 18 days, and are weaned at 21 days. **Diet** Grass roots, stems and seeds. **Habitat** Tall grasslands, mangroves, sand dunes, open forests with a grassy understorey, canefields and Hoop Pine plantations. **Traces** Spoil heaps and scats around burrow entrances. Scats are dark to light-brown, up to 5 mm across and 15 mm long, containing fine powdery particles. **Status** Common. **Head-body** 120-198 mm. **Tail** 78-190 mm. **Weight** 40-206 g.

R O D E N T S

148

Rattus colletti

Rattus tunneyi

Bush Rat

Rattus fuscipes

Widespread and abundant in the forest understorey of the coast and adjacent ranges, the Bush Rat has dense soft fur, grey to grey-brown or slightly reddish above, and grey or cream below. The tail is grey to brown, sparsely-haired with overlapping scales. The soles of the hindfeet are pale, distinguishing it from the Swamp Rat which has black soles. It has one pair of upper and lower gnawing incisor teeth and 3 pairs of molars on each side of the jaw. **Behaviour** Active at night, Bush Rats shelter by day in rock crevices, beneath fallen timber or in burrows 2-3 m long, often built under logs or stones. Burrows have a sloping, twisting tunnel leading to a vegetation-lined nest chamber some 150 mm diameter and 350-450 mm below ground. Adults live alone or with their young, and defend an exclusive home range of around 0.1-0.4 ha, although males roam over large areas in spring looking for females. Juveniles disperse and must establish a small home range with access to sufficient resources to survive the winter. **Development** Bush Rats are sexually mature at 3-4 months. They breed throughout the year with birth peaks in late spring and summer, and produce up to 4 litters per year. Females have 10 teats (sometimes 8 in the north) and give birth 20-21 days after mating. Litters usually comprise 4-5 young weighing about 5 g each. Their eyes are open by 3 weeks and they are weaned at 4-5 weeks. They have a life expectancy of up to 3 years, although in cooler climates few adults survive their first winter. **Diet** Insects, supplemented by fungi and other vegetation. **Habitat** Rainforests, heaths, sedgelands and wet sclerophyll forests with good ground cover of shrubs and ferns, to more than 1800 m. **Traces** Seed husks cracked lengthways. Scats are dark-brown, about 2-3 mm across and 5-15 mm long, with a pungent odour. **Status** Secure. **Head-body** 110-215 mm. **Tail** 105-195 mm. **Weight** 40-225 g. Males are much larger than females.

Long-haired Rat

Rattus villosissimus

This desert rodent is also known as the Plague Rat because its numbers reach plague proportions after several continuous wet years. The fur is long and grey above with conspicuous black guard hairs, and light grey below. The tail is grey to black with prominent dark hairs and overlapping scales. Like other rodents it has one pair of upper and lower gnawing incisor teeth and 3 pairs of molars on each side of the jaw. **Behaviour** Active mainly at night, Long-haired Rats shelter by day in burrows dug under bushes or rocks. Adult males are solitary and use several shallow, temporary burrows. Females live alone or with their young and construct complex breeding burrows to about 1 m deep and 3 m long, with several side passages and a central nesting chamber 100-150 mm diameter, containing a spherical nest of shredded vegetation. Burrows are grouped in grassy depressions with several well-worn runways between them. In plague years they wander in vast numbers over the countryside, invading camps and homesteads in their thousands before suddenly dying out after a few weeks. **Development** Females are sexually mature at about 10 weeks and have a very high reproductive potential. They breed throughout the year with lulls from mid-winter to early spring. Females have 12 teats and give birth to usually 6-7 blind young, born 21-23 days after mating. The young open their eyes at 17 days, and they are weaned at about 3 weeks. **Diet** Grasses, herbs, seeds and insects. In plagues they become cannibalistic and will attempt to eat any organic material. They need water and retreat to moist areas during droughts. **Habitat** Most habitats in arid to semi-arid areas with access to drinking water. **Traces** Spoil heaps at burrow entrances. **Status** Probably secure; vulnerable in NSW; rare and scattered except in plague years; threatened by stock disturbance of burrows. **Head-body** 120-225 mm. **Tail** 100-190 mm. **Weight** 105-290 g.

Rattus fuscipes

Rattus villosissimus

Cape York Rat

Rattus leucopus

A rainforest rodent found in Cape York and New Guinea, the Cape York Rat is divided into two distinct Australian populations separated by a wide, dry corridor around Laura. It has coarse, spiny fur, blackish-brown to golden-brown or reddish above and white or grey below. The head is pointed with large ears, sparsely covered with buff to reddish-brown hairs. The tail is slender and tapering, almost hairless, often mottled brown or grey, and has off-white patches in the most northerly Australian population. The pale hindfeet are stout and long. Like other rodents it has one pair of upper and lower gnawing incisor teeth and 3 pairs of molars on each side of the jaw. **Behaviour** Active mainly at night, Cape York Rats are ground-dwellers, foraging on the forest floor among the leaf litter and debris for insects and other foods. They shelter by day in burrows usually with several entrances hidden beneath the leaf litter, and a number of interconnecting chambers lined with dry leaves. Holes in tree bases and rotting logs are also used for shelter. Individuals may use more than one burrow and some burrows appear to be communal. **Development** Females are sexually mature at about 3 months. Cape York Rats breed throughout the year with a lull in the dry season from June to early September, and can produce up to 3 litters per year. Females have 6 (rarely 8) teats and usually give birth to 2-5 young, 21-24 days after mating. Their eyes are open by 22 days and they are weaned at about 25 days. **Diet** Insects, supplemented by fungi, herbs, seeds and fruit. **Habitat** Tropical rainforests. **Status** Probably secure. **Head-body** 130-215 mm. **Tail** 135-210 mm. **Weight** 70-215 g.

Canefield Rat

Rattus sordidus

The Canefield Rat is a rodent of the tropical grasslands and open forests, and is regarded as a serious pest by sugar cane growers who have created an ideal habitat for it. A short-limbed placental mammal, the Canefield Rat has coarse, spiny fur grizzled dark-brown to black above with prominent guard hairs, and light grey or buff belly fur. The tail is dark-brown to black with prominent overlapping scales. The soles of the hindfeet are pale, distinguishing it from the Swamp Rat, which has dark soles. Like other rodents it has one pair of upper and lower gnawing incisor teeth and 3 pairs of molars on each side of the jaw. **Behaviour** Canefield Rats are usually nocturnal, and forage in dense grass or sugar cane plantations with a complete canopy of leaves, but when population densities are high they are active during daylight hours. They rest in extensive burrow systems about 400 mm deep, with tunnels 50-100 mm diameter, sloping down to a nest chamber about 150 mm diameter lined with dry grass. Burrow entrances are near grass clumps, stones and stumps, and burrows are often concentrated in dense colonies with networks of runways between them. As many as 23 non-breeding adults have been found in one nest chamber, although females with young force other adults out. **Development** Females are sexually mature at 9-10 weeks, and breed at any time of year, with the majority of births occurring from March to May. Females have 12 teats and usually give birth to 6 young, 20-27 days after mating. Young are fully furred at 7 days, have their eyes open at 18 days, and are weaned at 3 weeks. Canefield Rats have the highest reproductive potential of all the native true rats, and may reach plague proportions in canefields. **Diet** Grass, seeds, leaves, sugar cane stems and insects. **Habitat** Tropical grasslands with dense ground cover, open forests, grassy clearings in rainforests, and canefields. **Traces** Scats are pale to dark brown, up to 5 mm across and 20 mm long, comprising powdery plant fragments. **Status** Secure. **Head-body** 123-210 mm. **Tail** 100-160 mm. **Weight** 50-260 g.

152

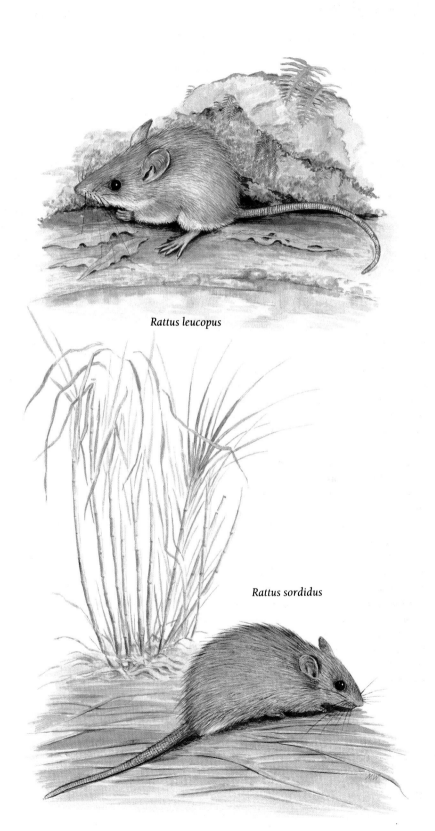

Rattus leucopus

Rattus sordidus

Black Rat
Rattus rattus

Introduced from Europe, the Black Rat has become well established in coastal Australia. It is a slender, gentle rodent with a sleek, smooth coat, charcoal-grey to black or light-brown above, and cream or white below. The head is long and pointed with large thin ears more 20 mm long, protruding eyes and long black whiskers. The tail is long and naked with overlapping scales. Like other rodents they have one pair of upper and lower gnawing incisor teeth and 3 pairs of molars on each side of the jaw. They may carry the plague bacillus and transmit other diseases to humans through their excreta. **Behaviour** Active mainly at night, Black Rats are agile climbers and good swimmers. They shelter in nests of shredded material in roofs, cavity walls, trees, shallow scrapes, or extensive shallow burrow systems, often around farm buildings or river banks. They are timid when cornered, but defend a territory against intruders, scent-marked by rubbing with the cheek or belly. Territorial groups establish a hierarchy with a dominant resident male and subordinates. Mated pairs share a nest until shortly before the female gives birth, when she excludes him. If disturbed the female moves her litter to a new nest. **Development** Sexually mature at 3-4 months, they live to about 12 months in the wild and breed throughout the year, producing up to 6 litters. Females have 10-12 teats and usually give birth to 4-10 young, 21-22 days after mating. Young are born blind and naked, and are weaned at about 28 days. **Diet** Grass stems and roots, seeds, insects, underground fungi, small mammals, birds and eggs. **Habitat** Disturbed areas, watercourses, urban areas and in buildings. **Traces** Fine, gnawed seed fragments and greasy smears where they brush past walls. Scats are usually dark-brown, 2-3 mm across and 5-15 mm long. **Status** Secure; regarded as a pest. **Head-body** 160-210 mm. **Tail** 180-255 mm. **Weight** 95-340 g.

Brown Rat
Rattus norvegicus

Introduced from Europe, the Brown Rat is a thickset placental mammal with shaggy, bristly fur, grey-brown above and white to grey below. The ears are small and rounded, close set and up to 20 mm long. The muzzle is blunt with long whiskers. The tail is stout, paler below, short and naked with overlapping scales. The pink hindfeet have long toes and pale soles. Like other rodents they have one pair of upper and lower gnawing incisor teeth and 3 pairs of molars on each side of the jaw. **Behaviour** Active mainly at night, Brown Rats can climb and swim well, but prefer to live at ground level, following odour trails along runways to food sources and nest sites. They shelter under bushes, rocks, in sewers and other urban sites, or construct extensive burrow systems, huddling together in nests of shredded material carried in the mouth. They hoard food in the nest, carrying it in their cheeks and manipulating it with their forefeet. Brown Rats often live in colonies of several hundred, recognising each other by smell and maintaining individual home ranges about 30 m across. Dominant males have exclusive territories around burrows containing several breeding females, and juveniles are forced to leave the colony. **Development** Sexually mature at 6-8 weeks, they are able to breed throughout the year, producing up to 5 litters per year. Females have 12 teats and give birth to 6-11 young, 21-23 days after mating. The young are well-furred at 10 days, open their eyes at about 15 days and can be weaned at 20 days. They seldom live more than 12 months. **Diet** Most plant and animal material. They kill and scavenge small mammals and nestlings, and eat bird's eggs. **Habitat** Degraded stream banks, rocky beaches, sewers, farm buildings and warehouses. **Traces** Spoil heaps at burrow entrances, nests under floors, gnawed seed fragments and greasy rub-marks beside runways. Scats are brown, about 3-5 mm across and 10-20 mm long. **Status** Secure; regarded as a pest. **Head-body** 180-260 mm. **Tail** 150-215 mm. **Weight** 200-480 g.

Rattus rattus

Rattus norvegicus

Fawn-footed Melomys

Melomys cervinipes

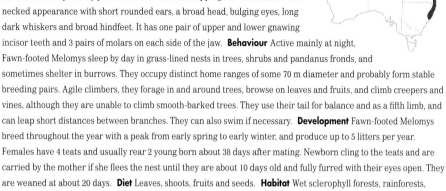

A rat-size placental mammal of the closed forests of eastern Australia, the Fawn-footed Melomys has long, soft, fine fur, sandy-brown to dark grey-brown or occasionally bright russet above, and white, cream or grey below. The naked tail is brown to black, partially prehensile with non-overlapping scales. It has a thick-necked appearance with short rounded ears, a broad head, bulging eyes, long dark whiskers and broad hindfeet. It has one pair of upper and lower gnawing incisor teeth and 3 pairs of molars on each side of the jaw. **Behaviour** Active mainly at night, Fawn-footed Melomys sleep by day in grass-lined nests in trees, shrubs and pandanus fronds, and sometimes shelter in burrows. They occupy distinct home ranges of some 70 m diameter and probably form stable breeding pairs. Agile climbers, they forage in and around trees, browse on leaves and fruits, and climb creepers and vines, although they are unable to climb smooth-barked trees. They use their tail for balance and as a fifth limb, and can leap short distances between branches. They can also swim if necessary. **Development** Fawn-footed Melomys breed throughout the year with a peak from early spring to early winter, and produce up to 5 litters per year. Females have 4 teats and usually rear 2 young born about 38 days after mating. Newborn cling to the teats and are carried by the mother if she flees the nest until they are about 10 days old and fully furred with their eyes open. They are weaned at about 20 days. **Diet** Leaves, shoots, fruits and seeds. **Habitat** Wet sclerophyll forests, rainforests, pandanus clumps, mangroves. **Traces** Scats are small dark-brown oval pellets about 2 mm across and 5 mm long, containing fine powdery plant matter. **Status** Common; vulnerable to rainforest clearing. **Head-body** 95-200 mm. **Tail** 115-210 mm. **Weight** 45-115 g.

Grassland Melomys

Melomys burtoni

A rat-size placental mammal, the Grassland Melomys is considered a pest by sugar cane farmers who have created new habitats for it by clearing forests. The fur is long and soft, grey-brown to reddish-brown or khaki above, sometimes pale orange on the flanks, and white, grey or cream below. It has a thick-necked appearance with short rounded ears, a broad head, bulging eyes, long whiskers and broad hindfeet. Its slender tail is partially prehensile, dark-brown and naked with small, non-overlapping scales. **Behaviour** Active at night, Grassland Melomys are agile climbers, foraging in tall reeds, sedges and sugar cane, using their partly prehensile tail for balance and grip. They can also cross waterways by swimming or rafting. They sleep by day in spherical nests of shredded leaves, bark and grass, 200-300 mm diameter, often with 2 entrances and usually about a metre above ground. Nests are woven around stout grass stems, built in shrubs, pandanus trees, hollow logs, under sheets of bark, and sometimes in short burrows. Males occupy home ranges of about 0.4 ha, females about 0.2 ha, and they become very aggressive if confined. **Development** Grassland Melomys breed throughout the year with peaks in the wet season in the Kimberley, in autumn and winter in Qld, and in spring and summer in the south (depending on the rainfall). Females have 4 teats and usually rear 2-3 young. Newborn develop rapidly and cling to the mother's teats until fully furred with their eyes open at 7-10 days old. They are carried by the mother if she changes nests, and are weaned at about 20 days. **Diet** Grass stems, seeds, berries, sugar cane and insects. **Habitat** Grasslands, sedgelands, heathlands, open forests, woodlands, vine thickets, monsoon forests, mangroves, and grassy clearings in rainforests. **Traces** Scats are pale to dark-brown cylindrical pellets about 2 mm across and up to 10 cm long, containing powdery plant material. **Status** Secure. **Head-body** 85-160 mm. **Tail** 90-175 mm. **Weight** 25-124 g.

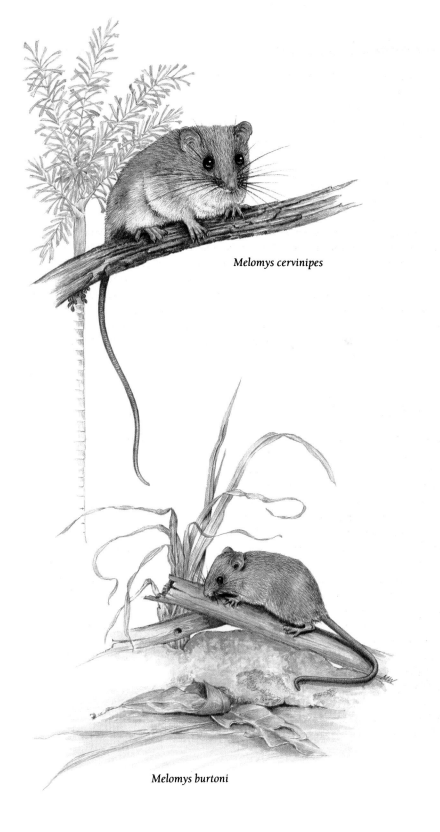

Melomys cervinipes

Melomys burtoni

Common Rock-rat
Zyzomys argurus

A compact rodent the size of a large mouse, the Common Rock-rat is found in rocky terrain with suitable nesting sites. It has coarse fur, golden-brown above and white below. Its sparsely-haired tail has overlapping scales and is swollen at the base with fat deposits. The skin of the tail is easily pulled off, and the tail withers away to a stump, hence many individuals have shortened or missing tails. The soles of the feet are smooth, the eyes are large and bulging, the ears rounded, and the muzzle has long whiskers. Like other rodents it has one pair of upper and lower gnawing incisor teeth and 3 pairs of molars on each side of the jaw. **Behaviour** Active at night, Common Rock-rats are very susceptible to heat stress and quickly die if exposed to the hot sun. They sleep in nests in cool refuges in rock crevices. Little is known about their behaviour. They fight ferociously when first caged together, and may establish dominance hierarchies in the wild. Few are seen towards the end of the wet season when they probably form breeding pairs. **Development** Sexually mature at 5-6 months, they may live to 2 years, and breed year round with a slight lull in the wet season. Females have 4 teats and rear 1-4 young, born about 35 days after mating. The young are left in the nest while the mother forages. They are fully-furred at 10 days, have their eyes open eyes at 12 days, and are independent at about 4 weeks. **Diet** Plant stems, leaves, seeds, grasses, fungi and insects. **Habitat** Woodlands, low open forests and grasslands, always in rocky areas, particularly sandstone country. **Traces** Scats are yellow to brown pellets, 2-3 mm across and up to about 8 mm long, containing fine particles of plant matter. **Status** Probably secure. **Head-body** 85-140 mm. **Tail** 90-125 mm. **Weight** 26-65 g.

Brush-tailed Tree-rat
Conilurus penicillatus

Also known as the Brush-tailed Rabbit-rat, this attractive rodent of tropical northern Australia and southern New Guinea is solidly built and has a rabbit-like appearance with very long ears, large bulging eyes, a broad, blunt head and elongated hind-feet. It has long coarse fur, light grizzled grey-brown above and creamy-white below. The tail is grey-brown at the base with a black or sometimes white brushy tip, and overlapping scales. Like other rodents it has one pair of upper and lower gnawing incisor teeth and 3 pairs of molars on each side of the jaw. **Behaviour** Active at night, Brush-tailed Tree-rats sleep by day in tree hollows, crevices, pandanus leaves and buildings. They nest in family groups comprising a male and female and her young. They are agile climbers and spend most of their time foraging for food in trees, climbing up to 15 m above the ground. They also forage on the ground where they are very agile and bound rapidly along with the tail held up, flicking from side-to-side. When disturbed they utter a threatening growl and climb the nearest tree. Other vocalisations include soft, high-pitched sounds. **Development** Brush-tailed Tree-rats have an extended breeding season lasting from March to October, timed to take advantage of food abundance during the late wet and mid dry seasons. Several litters are produced each season. Females have 4 teats and usually rear 3 young, born about 36 days after mating if she is not lactating, or 12 days later if she is lactating. Newborn are large and develop rapidly. They are fully-furred at 7 days, have their eyes open at 12 days and are weaned at about 20 days. Females can reproduce at only 6 weeks of age, although the average age is 11 weeks. They have a potential life span in captivity of 5 years. **Diet** Grass, herbs, seeds, fruits and termites. **Habitat** Open eucalypt forests and woodlands, rainforests, pandanus scrub, often on the seashore near large casuarina trees. **Traces** Scats are small oval pellets about 2 mm across and 5 mm long, light to dark brown, containing fine plant fragments. **Status** Probably secure. **Head-body** 135-227 mm. **Tail** 102-235 mm. **Weight** 102-242 g.

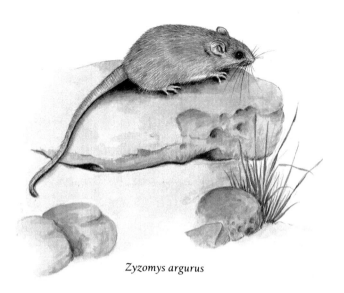

Zyzomys argurus

Conilurus penicillatus

Ash-grey Mouse

Pseudomys albocinereus

A small, attractive rodent, the Ash-grey Mouse is restricted to the semi-arid regions of southwestern Australia. It has long, soft fur, silver-grey tinged with fawn above, and white below. The nose, feet and tail are bright pink, the bulging eyes have prominent dark eyelashes, and the muzzle has long black or white whiskers. The ears are large and rounded, the tail slightly hairy with overlapping scales. Like other rodents it has one pair of upper and lower gnawing incisor teeth and 3 pairs of molars on each side of the jaw. **Behaviour** The Ash-grey Mouse is nocturnal, and forages on the ground at night for seeds and green vegetation, supplemented by insects in summer. During the day individuals or family groups, comprising a breeding pair and their growing young, sleep in a cool burrow up to 4 m long and about 600 mm below ground. Some burrows are complex with a number of interconnecting nesting chambers, side tunnels and a second entrance. **Development** The Ash-grey Mouse breeds in spring in the western part of its range. In eastern districts breeding takes place when food is available, with peaks after rain. Sexual maturity is reached at about 10 months. Females have 4 teats and usually rear 4 young born 37-38 days after mating. The young open their eyes at 15 days and are weaned at about 25 days. **Diet** Seeds, green vegetation, lichen and insects. It does not need access to drinking water, obtaining sufficient water from its food. **Habitat** Semi-arid tussock grasslands, tall shrublands, open sandplains with heath vegetation and woodlands. **Traces** Piles of excavated sand at burrow entrances. Scats are small round to oval pellets, about 2 mm across, containing fine plant fragments. **Status** Probably secure; vulnerable to land clearing. **Head-body** 63-110 mm. **Tail** 85-115 mm. **Weight** 21-40 g.

Plains Mouse

Pseudomys australis

One of Australia's most attractive rodents, the Plains Mouse is a desert species with a silver sheen to its soft, thick fur. It is sandy-brown to grey above and white to cream below, and is quite bulky with large ears, bulging eyes and a well-furred tail, brown or grey above and white below with a lighter tip. Like other rodents it has one pair of upper and lower gnawing incisor teeth and 3 pairs of molars on each side of the jaw. **Behaviour** Active mainly at night, Plains Mice sleep by day in cool, shallow burrows dug into the hard gibber, in claypans, swampy or sandy ground. Burrows are about 1 m long and up to 300 mm deep, with a single nest chamber often stuffed with vegetation. Temporary burrows are also used for shelter. Up to 20 adults may occupy a single burrow outside the breeding season, although when breeding a single male will share with 1-3 females. They gather in colonies occupying a group territory of about 1 ha with a number of burrows about 10 m apart, linked by a network of surface runways. They undergo large population fluctuations and colonies rapidly increase or decrease in size depending on food sources and predators. When alarmed they stand up on their hindlegs and squeal. They have a fairly extensive vocal repertoire of chirps, screeches and whistles. **Development** Females are sexually mature at about 3 months and breed mostly in winter and spring, probably after rain, sometimes rearing several litters in succession. Females have 4 teats and usually rear 3-4 young, born 30-31 days after mating. The young open their eyes at 15 days and are weaned at about 30 days. **Diet** Green plants, seeds and insects. They can survive without drinking. **Habitat** Arid gibber plains, ephemeral river flats, claypans, sandridges with low shrubs. **Traces** Scats are found along runways and around burrow entrances. They are brown, cylindrical to oval, about 2 mm across and 3-8 mm long, containing insect fragments or fine powdery particles. **Status** Vulnerable; threatened by Fox and Cat predation, habitat disturbance by sheep, and altered fire regimes. **Head-body** 100-140 mm. **Tail** 80-120 mm. **Weight** 50-80 g.

Pseudomys albocinereus

Pseudomys australis

New Holland Mouse

Pseudomys novaehollandiae

Easily confused with the House Mouse, but lacking its distinctive odour, this small placental mammal has larger ears and eyes, its tail is dusky brown above and white below, it sometimes has a dark stripe along the centre of its head, and females have only 4 teats. The fur is grey-brown often grizzled with long dark hairs above, and grey-white below. The feet are slender and covered with white hairs. Like other rodents it has one pair of upper and lower gnawing incisor teeth and 3 pairs of molars on each side of the jaw. **Behaviour** Active mainly at night, New Holland Mice live in family groups, sharing a permanent nest in a deep burrow up to 5 m long, with a nest chamber and a vertical entrance shaft concealed by shrubs or dead leaves. They also build short, shallow burrows, and use them as refuges to escape predators. They maintain separate home ranges, although those of adult females may overlap, and up to 17 animals per hectare may be found in good conditions. **Development** Females are sexually mature at 13 weeks, males at 20 weeks, and females can produce their first litter in the year of birth. The breeding season extends from August to January, with up to 4 litters of 2-6 (usually 4-5) young produced per year, born 32-39 days after mating. They open their eyes at 15 days, are weaned at 3-4 weeks, and may live 18-24 months. **Diet** Seeds, flowers, fungi, moss, roots and insects. **Habitat** Dry coastal heaths, scrubs, woodlands and open forests with a dense understorey, particularly in areas regenerating after fire. **Traces** Scats are deposited at burrow entrances, they are brown to dark-brown, 1-2 mm across and 2-5 mm long. **Status** Probably secure, but endangered in Vic. where isolated populations are dependent on appropriate fire regimes. **Head-body** 65-95 mm. **Tail** 79-110 mm. **Weight** 10-24 g.

Long-tailed Mouse

Pseudomys higginsi

Found only in Tasmania, the Long-tailed Mouse has very soft and dense fur forming a prominent ridge between the eyes. It is dark grey-brown above fading to fawn on the sides and grey white below, and has a very long, bicoloured tail, dark-grey above and white below, carried curved up well clear of the ground. The ears are large and round, the hindfeet are long and slender and clothed with white hairs. Like other rodents it has one pair of upper and lower gnawing incisor teeth and 3 pairs of molars on each side of the jaw. **Behaviour** Active mainly at night, Long-tailed Mice often forage by day in the winter, following runways and tunnels beneath the deep moss and forest debris. They sleep in nests of shredded bark or grass in a hole in a rotting stump or log; beneath leaf litter, or at the end of a short burrow. Placid, curious and highly sociable, they remain in a small home range and form permanent breeding pairs, sharing a nest with their offspring and defending a territory. Up to 10 families per hectare can be found in good conditions. They are good climbers, poor swimmers, leap randomly if threatened, and make a faint high-pitched whistle when disturbed. **Development** The breeding season extends from October to March, with 1-2 litters produced per year. Females have 4 teats and usually give birth to 3-4 young, born 31-32 days after mating. Newborn are well-furred and cling to their mother's teats or are left in the nest with the entrance temporarily plugged while the mother forages. If the mother is disturbed they cling to her teats and are dragged along behind her. They open their eyes at 15 days, are weaned at 25-30 days, leave the nest at about 3 months and may live to about 18 months. **Diet** Grass, seeds, fruits, insects and spiders. **Habitat** Wet closed forests with more than 2000 mm of rain per year. **Traces** Scats are dark-brown pellets about 3 mm across and 5 mm long, containing fine plant material. **Status** Probably secure. **Head-body** 115-150 mm. **Tail** 145-200 mm. **Weight** 50-90 g.

Pseudomys novaehollandiae

Pseudomys higginsi

Delicate Mouse

Pseudomys delicatulus

A tiny tropical species, the Delicate Mouse is Australia's smallest native rodent, and is easily killed if handled. Dainty and graceful in appearance, it has yellow-brown to grey-brown fur above and is white or cream below. The nose and feet are bright pink, and the tail is slender with overlapping scales. The ears are quite large and rounded (10-13 mm long), the eyes large and bulging. Like other rodents it has one pair of upper and lower gnawing incisor teeth and 3 pairs of molars on each side of the jaw. **Behaviour** Active mainly at night, the Delicate Mouse sleeps by day in a grass-lined nest in a burrow, termite mound, hollow log or under bark. In hard granite soils the burrows are short and shallow with false passages and a single nest chamber. In soft soil the burrows may be up to 400 mm deep with a single tunnel to 2 m long, terminating in a grass-lined spherical nest chamber. **Development** The Delicate Mouse reaches sexual maturity at 10-11 months, and usually mates in June and July, producing several litters in favourable conditions. Females have 4 teats and normally give birth to 3-4 young, born 28-31 days after mating. Newborn are about 25 mm long and weigh only 1 g. Their eyes open at 20 days, and they are fully-furred and weaned at 30 days. **Diet** Seeds of native grasses. **Habitat** Coastal sand dunes with sparse vegetation of grasses, herbs and stunted trees; low woodlands, open scrublands and hummock grasslands. **Traces** Spoil heaps to 100 mm high around burrow entrances. **Status** Probably secure; sparse, with marked seasonal population fluctuations. **Head-body** 55-75 mm. **Tail** 55-80 mm. **Weight** 6-15 g.

Western Chestnut Mouse

Pseudomys nanus

A small rodent of the tropical north of Australia, the Western Chestnut Mouse has short limbs, a stout body and small, round ears. The fur is light fawn-orange above with many long dark-brown hairs, light orange-brown on the flanks, and white on the belly. It has a pronounced light eye ring, and a naked tail with overlapping scales. Like other rodents it has one pair of upper and lower gnawing incisor teeth and 3 pairs of molars on each side of the jaw. **Behaviour** Despite its abundance, little information is available about the lifestyle of the Western Chestnut Mouse. It is known to be active at night, and to sleep by day in a grass nest. In captivity they fight each other and make frequent high-pitched whistling calls when active. **Development** Western Chestnut Mice breed most of the year except in the dry season (September and November). Their habitat is subject to fires and flooding, and they probably rear several litters in rapid succession to take advantage of good conditions. Females have 4 teats and usually give birth to 3 young born 22-24 days after mating. The young are furred at 7 days, have their eyes open at 12 days and are weaned at about 21 days. **Diet** Native grasses and seeds. They may be able to survive without drinking. **Habitat** Woodlands, tropical tussock grasslands and open forests with good ground cover on rocky or sandy soil. **Status** Secure. **Head-body** 80-140 mm. **Tail** 70-140 mm. **Weight** 25-50 g.

Pseudomys delicatulus

Pseudomys nanus

Sandy Inland Mouse

Pseudomys hermannsburgensis

The Sandy Inland Mouse is a slender, slightly-built rodent, very similar in appearance to the introduced House Mouse, although it lacks the latter's distinctive musty smell, and has larger ears, eyes and tail. The fur is sandy-brown to grey above, grading to white below. Like other rodents it has one pair of upper and lower gnawing incisor teeth and 3 pairs of molars on each side of the jaw. **Behaviour** Active mainly at night, the Sandy Inland Mice sleep in a grass-lined nest in a cool, deep burrow near the base of a shrub or tree. Burrows have a single tunnel up to 1 m long extending about 500 mm below the surface. They are gregarious and share burrows, although social tolerance depends on their breeding condition. Small groups of 4-6 breeding adults have been found in the same burrow, and 22 non-breeding adults in another burrow. Pregnant or lactating females become intolerant of other adults and have been recorded castrating or killing their mates. They forage mostly on the ground and will climb into shrubs and trees searching for food, climbing up to 1 m above the ground. **Development** Sexually mature at about 3 months, they breed after good rainfall, and produce several litters in favourable conditions. Females have 4 teats and normally give birth to 3-4 blind, naked young, 30-34 days after mating. At 20 days they are well-furred with their eyes open, and are independent at 30 days. **Diet** Seeds, roots, tubers, grass and insects. They can survive without drinking. **Habitat** Woodlands, mallee shrublands, hummock grasslands, gibber plains and alluvial flats. **Traces** Scats and piles of soil at burrow entrances. Scats are tiny brown pellets about 1 mm across and 3 mm long, containing fine plant fragments. **Status** Secure; vulnerable in NSW where it competes with stock and feral animals; undergoes large population fluctuations. **Head-body** 65-85 mm. **Tail** 70-90 mm. **Weight** 8-15 g.

Forrest's Mouse

Leggadina forresti

Distinguished by its short stumpy tail, plump body, and blunt muzzle with many long whiskers, Forrest's Mouse is a small placental mammal of the arid regions of Australia. The fur is thick, coarse and shiny, yellow-brown to grey above with scattered dark hairs, and pure white on the belly and feet. The tail is grey above and white below with overlapping scales. The pinkish-grey ears are short and rounded, the eyes large and bulging. Like other rodents it has one pair of upper and lower gnawing incisor teeth and 3 pairs of molars on each side of the jaw.

Behaviour Active at night, Forrest's Mice sleep during the heat of the day in grass-lined nests in shallow burrows 150-800 mm deep, or in cracks in the soil. Burrows are about 400 mm long with several blind tunnels and a single nest chamber. Forrest's Mice have no fixed home range and often travel more than 1 km overnight looking for food. Adults live alone or with their young, and females with young are intolerant of other adults. **Development** Forrest's Mice breed after rainfall, and may rear several litters in succession in favourable conditions. Females have 4 teats and normally give birth to 3-4 young, probably 20-30 days after mating. The young are well-furred by 10 days, have their eyes open at 20 days, and are weaned at 28 days. **Diet** Seeds, green vegetation, beetles and spiders. They can survive without drinking. **Habitat** Arid and semi-arid areas including tussock grasslands, low shrublands, mulga woodlands, monsoon forests, sand plains and clay pans. **Status** Vulnerable; threatened by grazing stock. **Head-body** 65-105 mm. **Tail** 50-75 mm. **Weight** 15-30 g.

Pseudomys hermannsburgensis

Leggadina forresti

RODENTS

House Mouse

Mus musculus

One of the most adaptable placental mammals in the world, the House Mouse probably originated in central Asia and accompanied humans to Australia. The fur is soft and dense, to 7 mm long, brownish-grey above and white to grey or pale-yellow below. The ears are large and rounded, the eyes bulging, and the tail sparsely-haired with overlapping scales. It can be distinguished from other small rodents by its distinctive musty smell and a notch on the inner surface of the upper incisor teeth. **Behaviour** Active mainly at night, House Mice sleep in spherical nests of shredded material in secluded sites in buildings, reed beds, cracks in the ground, or at the centre of complex shallow burrow systems with several narrow tunnels and entrances. In buildings they live in small family groups and defend a fixed territory about 6 m diameter, although juveniles are forced to disperse. Less defined territorial behaviour is exhibited in the wild. Movements are unhurried, although they can move quickly and climb easily using their sharp claws. They are poor swimmers and become torpid in cold conditions. **Development** Sexually mature at 6-8 weeks, they usually breed from October to April, but in good years they can breed year-round. Females have 10 teats and may rear up to 11 litters of 4-10 young per year. Females mate soon after giving birth, the embryo remaining dormant for up to 18 days if she is lactating. Pregnancy lasts 19-21 days, infants open their eyes at 12 days and are weaned at 18 days. **Diet** Seeds, fruits, fungi, insects and household scraps. **Habitat** Most habitats, from deserts to wet coastal areas, but is displaced by small native mammals. **Traces** Distinctive musty odour. Scats are 1-2 mm across and 3-5 mm long, musty smelling, and often deposited in dark corners. **Status** Secure; regarded as a pest; occasionally reaches plague proportions. **Head-body** 60-100 mm. **Tail** 75-100 mm. **Weight** 8-25 g.

Mitchell's Hopping-mouse

Notomys mitchellii

Distinguished by its long hindlegs and bipedal hopping gait, Mitchell's Hopping-mouse is fawn to dark-grey above, often grizzled, and grey-white below. A wide tract of shiny white hairs runs from the throat to chest. The tail is brown or grey above and lighter below with a brush of dark hairs at the tip. The ears are long and oval-shaped with sparse brown hairs outside. Like other rodents it has one pair of upper and lower gnawing incisor teeth and 3 pairs of molars on each side of the jaw. **Behaviour** Active at night, Mitchell's Hopping-mice shelter by day in a nest of grass or shredded vegetation in a deep burrow system (hollow logs are used in mallee woodlands). The nest chamber is at the end of a broad horizontal tunnel around 100-150 mm diameter and 1.5 m below ground, accessed by several vertical shafts (pop-holes) dug from below. Mixed groups of up to 8 adults build adjacent burrow systems up to 150 m apart. Each group uses several burrows and individuals may share a burrow to maintain a high humidity and reduce water loss in desert conditions. Secretions from glands on the neck and chest are thought to be used to mark home ranges and members of the colony. They move with a bipedal hopping gait, which uses less energy than running. **Development** Sexually mature at about 3 months, they probably breed throughout the year in favourable conditions, rearing litters of 1-4 young. Pregnancy lasts 37-40 days, and the newborn cling tightly to the mother's teats and are dragged behind her when she moves. They are well-furred at 7 days, open their eyes at 20 days, are weaned at 30-35 days, and live for up to 5 years in captivity. **Diet** Mostly seeds and fruit, supplemented by flowers, leaves, stems and insects. **Habitat** Semi-arid mallee woodlands, dry heaths, dunefields and shrublands. **Traces** Scats are deposited near burrows and runways. They are small pellets, 1-2 mm across and about 5 mm long, containing fine plant fragments. **Status** Probably secure; extinct in NSW; vulnerable to land clearing. **Head-body** 100-130 mm. **Tail** 140-160 mm. **Weight** 40-60 g.

Mus musculus

Notomys mitchellii

Fawn Hopping-mouse

Notomys cervinus

Found in the arid gibber plains of central Australia, the Fawn Hopping-mouse has long hindlegs, a distinctive bipedal hopping gait and a long, tufted tail. The fur is pale pinkish-fawn to grey above and white below. Males have a small, naked, raised, flat glandular area on the chest, often stained by pale-yellow flaky secretions in sexually active animals. The ears are long, rounded and sparsely-haired. Like other rodents they have one pair of upper and lower gnawing incisor teeth and 3 pairs of molars on each side of the jaw. **Behaviour** Active at night, Fawn Hopping-mice shelter during the day in simple, cool, humid burrows with 1-3 entrances. Burrows in gibber plains are up to 1 m deep and have up to 4 occupants. In hard claypans they are up to 300 mm deep and have up to 7 occupants. They live in family groups and forage alone within a few hundred metres of the burrow. Fawn Hopping-mice are more aggressive than other hopping-mice, but avoid sandy areas which are the domain of the Dusky Hopping Mouse. The male's chest gland is probably used to scent-mark group members or areas within its home range. **Development** Sexually mature at about 6 months, they are opportunistic breeders, probably reproducing after periods of good rainfall, and undergoing periodic population increases. Females rear litters of usually 3 young born 38-43 days after mating, although pregnancy may be prolonged by up to 11 days if she is still suckling the previous litter. Newborn cling to the mother's teats and are dragged around by her if disturbed. They are well-furred at birth, have their eyes open at about 21 days, and are weaned at 4 weeks. **Diet** Seeds, green plant matter and some insects. They will drink salty water, and can survive without drinking. **Habitat** Gibber plains, tussock grasslands and low shrublands with hard clay and stony soils. **Status** Vulnerable; now extinct in NSW; threatened by grazing stock and Cat predation. **Head-body** 95-120 mm. **Tail** 105-160 mm. **Weight** 30-50 g.

Spinifex Hopping-mouse

Notomys alexis

With its long hindlegs, bipedal hopping gait and long tufted tail, the Spinifex Hopping-mouse is a small, distinctive, placental mammal of the arid zone. The short fur is light-brown to chestnut above and grey-white below. Both sexes have a small throat pouch of unknown function. All males and some females have a naked glandular area on the chest. The ears are long, rounded and sparsely-haired. Like other rodents they have one pair of upper and lower gnawing incisor teeth and 3 pairs of molars on each side of the jaw. **Behaviour** Active at night, Spinifex Hopping-mice shelter in deep, humid burrows from the heat of the day. Burrows are up to 1 m below ground, and have several vertical shafts connected to a broad horizontal tunnel leading to a nest chamber lined with twigs, grass or shredded vegetable matter. They are highly social and 10 adults may share a burrow, plugging the entrance with sand to reduce evaporative water loss. Groups build adjacent burrow systems linked by runways, and cooperate in digging, rearing young and rejecting strangers. Secretions from the chest gland are probably used to scent-mark group members. They use a quadrupedal gait when moving slowly, but bound on their long hindfeet with their brush-tipped tail trailing behind when moving fast. **Development** Sexually mature at about 8 weeks, they can reproduce at any time of year, with peaks in spring and after periods of good rainfall. Pairs lock during copulation and often struggle violently or turn back-to-back before separating. Females have 4 teats and rear litters of up to 6 (usually 3-4) young, born 32-34 days after mating (although pregnancy may last 40 days if the mother is suckling 4 or more young). Young are left in the nest while the mother forages, and may be retrieved by any adult if they stray. They have their eyes open at about 20 days, are weaned at 4 weeks, and live for up to 4 years in captivity. **Diet** Seeds, leaves, roots and insects. They can survive without drinking. **Habitat** Arid spinifex and tussock grasslands, woodlands, shrublands and desert sand dunes. **Traces** Scats are small brown pellets, about 2 mm across and 5 mm long, contain fine plant particles, and are scattered near burrows and runways. **Status** Secure, with marked population fluctuations. **Head-body** 90-115 mm. **Tail** 115-150 mm. **Weight** 28-50 g.

Notomys cervinus

Notomys alexis

Common Dolphin

Delphinus delphis

Commonly seen in Australian coastal waters, this torpedo-shaped marine mammal is dark grey to purple-black above, and cream to white below, with a distinctive hourglass pattern on its flanks. The tips of the snout, lower jaw and lips are purplish-black, and the eyes have black patches around them. It has a long slender beak, a slender, sickle-shaped dorsal fin, thin tapering flippers, and thin tail flukes with a slight notch in the edge. The jaws have 40-58 pairs of small teeth.

Behaviour Sociable, friendly and playful, Common Dolphins move in groups of 5-50 and occasionally congregate in herds of 3000 or more, following the movements of schools of migrating fish. Small feeding groups scatter in the late afternoons to feed on food organisms rising to the surface, and return to the herd to rest or play. They can dive to 280 m, stay underwater for 8 minutes or more, and are often seen playing in the bow-waves of ships. They communicate over long distances using various pulsed sounds including squawks, squeaks, yaps and shrill whistles. In dark and murky waters they use echo-location to navigate and find prey.

Development Females are sexually mature at 3-4 years, males at 7-12 years, and they have a lifespan of 20-22 years. Common Dolphins mate in spring and autumn at intervals of 1-3 years. A single calf, 700-900 cm long, is born 10-11 months later, and is suckled by the mother for 1-3 years. **Diet** They are opportunistic predators of fish and cephalopods, including herrings, anchovies, sardines and squid. **Habitat** Warm temperate, sub-tropical and tropical coastal waters and deep offshore oceanic waters, generally between 10° and 28°C. **Status** Secure; protected in Australian waters. **Length** 1.7-2.4 m. **Weight** 50-136 kg.

Bottlenose Dolphin

Tursiops truncatus

A coastal, torpedo-shaped marine mammal, the Bottlenose Dolphin is dark or light-grey above, grading to light-grey on the flanks, and white or pink below with a blue-grey band from the base of the beak to each eye. The head is robust with a relatively short beak with 18-26 pairs of teeth in each jaw. The lower jaw extends beyond the upper jaw and curves up slightly. The flippers are pointed, the dorsal fin is sickle-shaped, and the tail flukes are thin with rounded tips and a notched edge. **Behaviour** Friendly and playful, Bottlenose Dolphins usually swim close to shore and rise to breathe every 15-20 seconds, but can remain submerged for several minutes, particularly when surf-riding, They swim in pods of 5-20, forming part of a herd of several hundred, and communicate over long distances using pulsed sounds including squawks, squeaks, yaps and shrill whistles. Females whistle almost continually for several days after giving birth to give an acoustic imprint to their young. In dark and murky waters they use echo-location to navigate and detect prey, and if threatened will chase off and sometimes kill a shark. Herds have a home range of around 85 sq km, while individual home ranges vary from 15 to 40 sq km, according to age and sex. Breeding females form relatively stable groups, and group members will care for another mother's infant while she feeds. Subadult males associate in bachelor groups. **Development** Males are sexually mature at 10-14 years, females at 5-12 years, and they live to 40 years or more. Females may produce 8 offspring during their lives, giving birth at 2-3 year intervals. Calves are born 12 months after mating, from February to May and September to November. Newborn are 900-1300 cm long, and suckle for 12-18 months. **Diet** They are opportunistic predators of a wide variety of marine organisms including fish, squid, eels and crustaceans. **Habitat** Warm-temperate, subtropical and tropical coastal waters, bays and estuaries, occasionally ascending the tidal reaches of rivers. **Status** Secure; protected in Australian waters. **Length** 2.3-4 m. **Weight** 150-650 kg.

Delphinus delphis

Tursiops truncatus

Australian Sea-lion

Neophoca cinerea

The only sea-lion endemic to Australia, this marine mammal has a bulky, streamlined body with a blunt snout and a Dog-like head, with long whiskers and a very small, rolled, external ear. Adult males are rich chocolate-brown to blackish with a long mane of white hair over the neck. Adult females and young are silver-grey to fawn above, and yellow to cream below. They have flippers instead of fore-limbs. The hindlegs are webbed and face the rear. **Behaviour** Active by day, Australian Sea-lions forage along the edge of the continental shelf, generally staying within 300 km of their birthplace. They are powerful swimmers, diving, leaping out of the water, and surfing onto beaches, obtaining most thrust from their foreflippers. They can also gallop and climb cliffs, and male Sea-lions have been found 10 km inland. Sea journeys tend to be short, and throughout the year they congregate at their tra-ditional breeding grounds. Some colonies comprise more than 500 animals, but the majority are much smaller. Numbers peak during and after the pupping season, when dominant males establish territories, fighting and threat-ening other males with loud growls, barks and roars. Pregnant females come ashore about 3 days before giving birth in rocky crevices and gullies. They are then herded by males into their territories, the strongest, most dominant males maintaining the largest harems. **Development** Females are sexually mature at about 3 years and breed every 17-18 months, producing a single pup from October to January. They mate 4-9 days after giving birth, although the embryo remains dormant for about 4 months, and takes another 14-15 months to develop. Newborn are 600-750 mm long and weigh 6-8 kg. They have thick, soft fur, moult at 2 months, swim at 3 months and suckle for 12 months or more. The mother stays with the pup for 2 weeks, then leaves it in a sheltered place while she feeds at sea, return-ing every 2 days or so. They have a lifespan of 12 years or more. **Diet** Squid, crayfish, fish, cephalopods and pen-guins. **Habitat** Cool-temperate coastal waters, isolated sandy beaches and rocky coastlines. **Status** Endangered; protected; sensitive to human disturbance. **Length** Males 1.85-2.5 m; females 1.3-1.8 m. **Weight** Males to 300 kg; females 60-105 kg.

Dugong

Dugong dugon

The Dugong is the only herbivorous marine mammal. It has a bulky, streamlined body, grey to bronze above and lighter below, with fine scattered hairs; older animals have large white patches. It has paddle-like forelimbs and a horizontal tail-fluke instead of hindlimbs. It has a broad, flat head, small eyes, small ear-openings, a large mouth with fleshy lips, short bristles on the muzzle, and nostrils on the top of the head which close when diving. Males have a pair of protruding, tusk-like upper incisors. **Behaviour** Dugongs spend their lives in the water, feeding close to shore dur-ing daylight hours and travelling about 25 km daily. They dive repeatedly for food, staying underwater for up to 8.5 minutes (average 76 seconds), swimming at up to 22 kph with vertical strokes of their tail-flukes, using their flippers to change direction and brake. Active and alert, they live alone or in small family groups, sometimes con-gregating in herds of several hundred, and show no evidence of large-scale migration. Females give birth in shallow water to avoid sharks. They have good vision and hearing, and communicate with whistling and chirping sounds. **Development** Sexually mature at 9-15 years, they mate from May to November at 3-6 year intervals, giving birth to a single young 12-14 months later. Females have 2 teats in the armpits and males have internal testes. Calves weigh 20-35 kg, are 1-1.25 m long, and ride on the mother's back when not suckling, staying with her for about 2 years. Dugongs have a lifespan of up to 73 years. **Diet** Seagrasses, supplemented with algae. **Habitat** Shallow tropical coastal waters and estuaries. **Status** Vulnerable; threatened by hunting, coastal pollution, habitat destruction and incidental capture in fishing nets. **Length** 2.5-3.3 m. **Weight** 250-450 kg.

Neophoca cinerea

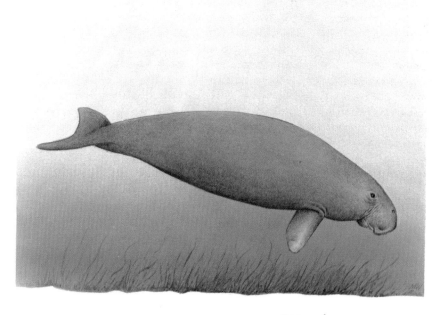

Dugong dugon

SEA MAMMALS

New Zealand Fur-seal

Arctocephalus forsteri

The New Zealand Fur-seal is a streamlined marine mammal with a Dog-like head, pointed snout with long whiskers and a small, rolled, external ear. It is dark grey-brown above and lighter below. Bulls have a massive neck and a thick mane of coarse hair. Newborn are black and moult at 2 months to become silver-grey. They have strong flippers and webbed hindlegs facing the rear. **Behaviour** New Zealand Fur-seals rest, moult and breed on land, where they move with a slow, shuffling walk. They are powerful swimmers, propelling themselves with vertical strokes of their webbed hindlimbs. Breeding colonies of up to 1300 begin to form in October, when bulls join cows and juveniles on exposed shores of offshore islands. Chosen sites include rock slopes and ledges, boulder-strewn beaches and caves. The most powerful bulls establish an individual territory among the females by posturing, guttural barking or savage fighting, and defend a harem of about 6 cows. Unsuccessful bulls and young males congregate on the edge of the breeding area. Bulls leave in late January and swim off to hauling grounds on rocky beaches. **Development** Sexually mature at 4-6 years, males only breed when strong enough to defend a territory at about 10 years of age. Births occur from November to January and the cows mate 8 days after giving birth to a single pup. The embryo remains dormant for some 4 months and takes another 8 months to develop. The newborn are about 450 mm long and weigh some 4 kg. The mother goes to sea to feed 10 days after giving birth, returning 3-5 days later to suckle for 2-4 days before leaving again. Pups congregate in pods and are suckled for 9-10 months. **Diet** Squid, fish, octopus, rock lobster, crab and some seabirds. **Habitat** Cool temperate coastal waters and offshore islands with rocky beaches. **Status** Probably secure; relatively abundant in New Zealand; protected in Australia. **Length** Males 1.5-2.5 m; females 1-1.5 m. **Weight** Males 120-200 kg; females 35-70 kg.

Australian Fur-seal

Arctocephalus pusillus

The largest and most abundant seal in Australia, this streamlined marine mammal has a Dog-like head with long whiskers and a small, rolled external ear. Bulls are dark grey-brown with a mane of long coarse hair. Cows are silver-grey with a creamy-yellow throat and chest, and a chocolate-brown abdomen. Pups are dark-brown above, yellowish below and moult at 3 months. They have flippers for forelimbs and webbed hindlegs facing the rear. **Behaviour** Australian Fur-seals rest, moult and breed on land, where they move with a slow shuffling walk or a fast gallop. They swim with vertical strokes of their webbed hindlimbs and can dive to at least 200 m. They have good underwater vision but poor vision on land, and may use echo-location underwater. Breeding grounds are occupied year-round by females and juveniles. Bulls arrive to breed in late October and the most powerful reoccupy territories by roaring, barking and fighting off intruding bulls. At times they may acquire a harem of 60 or more cows; while unsuccessful bulls and bachelor males congregate on the periphery. Males disperse to feed at sea in January. **Development** Sexually mature at 4-5 years, males only breed when they are strong enough to defend a territory at 8-13 years old, until they are defeated 3-6 years later. Females begin breeding at 3-6 years, give birth from October to late December and mate 5-7 days later. The embryo remains dormant for 3-4 months and takes another 9 months to develop. Newborn are 600-700 mm long and weigh 4-13 kg. Pups congregate in pods and the cows go to sea after mating, returning weekly to suckle their pups for a further 8 months. They then accompany her at sea until weaned by 12 months, and have a lifespan of 19-21 years. **Diet** Squid, fish, octopus and rock lobsters. **Habitat** Cool temperate coastal waters, rocky coastlines. **Status** Probably secure; protected in Australia. **Length** Males 2-2.3 m; females 1.2-1.7 m. **Weight** Males 218-360 kg; females 36-113 kg.

Arctocephalus forsteri

Arctocephalus pusillus

Leopard Seal

Hydrurga leptonyx

A summer inhabitant of the outer fringes of the Antarctic pack-ice, this streamlined marine mammal moves into Australian coastal waters in winter. It has a reptilian-like head with wide gaping jaws and a narrow neck. Its long, slim body is dark-grey above and lighter below with grey or black spots on the sides and throat. Juveniles have a dark stripe on their back and dark spots below. It lacks an external ear and has distinctive 3-pronged cheek teeth. It has flippers for forelimbs, and the webbed hindlegs are turned backwards to act as tail flukes for underwater propulsion.

Behaviour Leopard Seals rest, moult and breed on land, heaving their whole body forward in a caterpillar-like motion. In the water they are fast and powerful swimmers, propelled by vertical strokes of their webbed hindlimbs. They are generally solitary, living on the outer fringes of the Antarctic pack-ice, and forming monogamous breeding pairs in summer. Young seals disperse north in winter, and some reach the coast of Australia between July and October, venturing as far north as Heron Island. They have a vocal repertoire of gurgles, grunts, chirps and whistles, and a throaty alarm call. **Development** Females are sexually mature at 2-7 years, males at 3-6 years. They mate from January to March after weaning their young. The embryo remains dormant for some 3 months and takes another 7-8 months to develop. A single pup, 1.1-1.5 m long, is born from September to January and is suckled for about 4 weeks. **Diet** Krill, fish, cephalopods, seabirds and the young of other seals. They toss penguins around, biting off the flesh and leaving the skin. **Habitat** Pack ice, Antarctic coastline, subantarctic islands, cold to temperate coastal waters. **Status** Secure; protected. **Length** Females to 3.6 m; males to 3 m. **Weight** Females to 450 kg; males to 270 kg.

Humpback Whale

Megaptera novaeangliae

A huge but friendly marine mammal, the Humpback Whale is grey-black above and black and white below, with a humpback and a broad, round, flattened head. Barnacle-encrusted knobs protrude from its jaw, and on each side of the roof of the mouth hang 270-400 fringed sheets of a horny material (baleen) used to sieve krill from the water. Its flippers are up to 16 m long have knobs on their trailing edges, and the dorsal fin varies from a small protuberance to a sickle-shaped fin.

Behaviour Humpback Whales can swim at 20 kph and dive for 30 minutes, surfacing for 3-6 minutes between dives, often leaping out of the water and rolling in mid-air. They use echo-location to navigate in murky waters, and migrate annually from their summer feeding grounds in the Southern ocean to tropical waters to calve and mate, leaving in May and returning in November. One population migrates up Australia's west coast and another follows the east coast. Females with calves and immatures make the journey first, followed by adult males, then non-pregnant cows, with pregnant cows arriving last. Males advertise their arrival in the breeding area by singing a song of cries, yups and chirps, lasting 6-35 minutes, repeated day and night. Males of the same population all sing variations of the same song, which changes each year. They form social groups with up to 7 members and often fight over females. **Development** Sexually mature at 4-5 years, they live to 50 years or more. Females produce a single calf every 2-3 years, giving birth from June to October, 11-11.5 months after mating. Calves are 4-5 m long, weigh up to 2 tonnes, and are expert swimmers. They suckle for 5-7 months, drinking about 600 litres of fatty milk daily, pumped from huge mammary glands at the base of the mother's pectoral fins. Calves swim with their mother for 2-3 years. **Diet** Antarctic Krill, supplemented by other swimming crustaceans. **Habitat** Coastal waters. **Status** Endangered; protected internationally. **Length** 11-15 m. **Weight** to about 65 tonnes.

Hydrurga leptonyx

Megaptera novaeangliae

Dingo

Canis familiaris

The dingo was introduced to Australia 3500-11,000 years ago, and has colonised most of the mainland. It is a form of the Domestic Dog, and was probably derived from a small Indian Wolf 10,000-12,000 years ago. Dingoes are typically ginger to sandy-brown with white points, although some are black with sandy-brown markings. The ears are held erect, the snout is narrower than the Domestic Dog, while the canine teeth are larger and more slender. They have a bushy tail with a scent gland at the base. The legs are slender with 5 toes on the forefeet and 4 on the hindfeet. The claws are straight and non-retractable. Dingoes interbreed with Domestic Dogs, and wild populations often include hybrids. **Behaviour** Dingoes are active mainly around dawn and dusk, with bursts of activity throughout the day and night. During the heat of the day they shelter in a cave or shady spot. Females rear their young in a den in a cave, rock pile, hollow log or in an enlarged Rabbit warren or wombat burrow, usually within 3 km of water. They are intelligent and secretive animals and although they act independently, they belong to loose associations, integrated and distinguished from other groups by scent-marking. They hunt alone for small game and cooperate to hunt larger game such as kangaroos and cattle, forming packs with a dominant male and female and 4-5 subordinates (usually offspring of previous matings between the dominant pair). They rarely fight, maintaining hierarchies by ritualised postures.Dingoes are not territorial, although they usually remain in a well-defined home range, which may be some 20 km across, varying in size according to the terrain and abundance of prey. Short term associations are formed during the breeding season. Non-breeding yearlings often help the parents to rear their young, standing guard and coaching them in hunting techniques.Dingoes do not bark, but howl to keep contact with others when hunting and to attract mates during the breeding season. A howl-bark is used as an alarm signal. **Development** Females are sexually mature at 1-4 years of age, males at 2-4 years. They breed once a year and give birth to 2-9 pups from March to September, 63 days after mating. Newborn are blind and well-furred, and are mobile by about 4 weeks. The mother suckles her pups for 3-4 months, after that she fetches and regurgitates water and provides food until they are able to hunt. If food is scarce they are moved to another den, and the mother may change den sites frequently. Juveniles often follow their parents until about 12 months old. **Diet** An opportunistic predator, mammals are their most important food source, supplemented by reptiles, birds and even insects. Rodents and Rabbits are the most common prey in central Australia, and macropods constitute the major part of the diet in southeastern Australia. They are able to survive for long periods without drinking, obtaining sufficient water from their prey. **Habitat** Most habitats including arid and semi-arid areas with access to drinking water. In southeastern Australia they prefer the margins of forests bordering on heathlands and grasslands. **Traces** Bones and feathers near den entrance. Scats are often deposited on rocks and grass tussocks. They are up to 4 cm across, and 10 cm long, often twisted with tufts of hair at one end, and contain bone fragments. **Status** Secure. **Head-body** 860-980 m. **Tail** 260-380 mm. **Weight** 9.5-19.5 kg.

Canis familiaris

Bat Structure

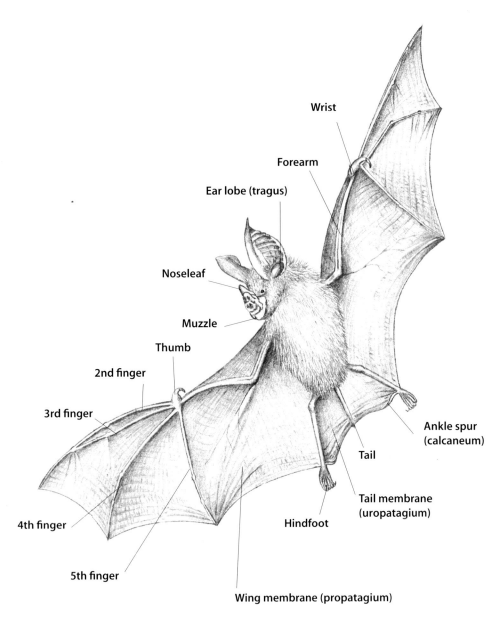

Wrist

Forearm

Ear lobe (tragus)

Noseleaf

Muzzle

Thumb

2nd finger

3rd finger

4th finger

5th finger

Wing membrane (propatagium)

Hindfoot

Tail

Tail membrane (uropatagium)

Ankle spur (calcaneum)

Acknowledgements

A number of people gave much of their time and expertise in the preparation of this book, and I would like to express my special thanks to the staff of the Australian Museum; in particular to Linda Gibson, who facilitated access to the museum's collection of mammals and made constructive criticism of the illustrations; to Tim Flannery, who checked the distribution maps; to Tish Ennis; and to the staff of the library who put in a great deal of legwork on my behalf. Many thanks to Ray Williams who gave unstintingly of his time and knowledge, and was of immeasurable help with reference material. Thanks to Steven Waterhouse, a keen young naturalist, who sought out illustrative reference works with unbounded enthusiasm, and to Colin Gudgeon who also helped with reference material. Thanks to the staff of Macquarie University Fauna Park; the staff of Featherdale Wildlife Park; and the staff of Koala Park.

Index